PUBLIC ARCHITECTURE
THE ART INSIDE

PUBLIC ARCHITECTURE
THE ART INSIDE

Curtis Fentress

In conversation with

Mary Voelz Chandler

ORO editions

contents

To Begin.. vii
Biography.. viii
Curtis Fentress | On Architecture... ix
Design and Function Meet in Public Architecture | John Morris Dixon........................... xii
Curtis Fentress & the Architecture of Experience | Michael McCoy............................... xiv

airports 1

Introduction... 2
Denver International Airport... 4
Incheon International Airport.. 22
Los Angeles International Airport... 34
San Jose International Airport.. 48
Seattle-Tacoma International Airport.. 56
Raleigh-Durham International Airport.. 62
Fashion + Airports 🜊.. 68

convention centers 2

Introduction... 74
Colorado Convention Center.. 76
Pasadena Convention Center... 88
Palm Springs Convention Center.. 100
Santa Fe Community Convention Center.. 110
Sculpture + Public Buildings 🦎.. 120

museums 3

Introduction... 126
National Museum of the Marine Corps.. 128
National Cowboy and Western Heritage Museum................................... 142
National Museum of Wildlife Art... 152
Museum of Science | Boston.. 162
Museums + Inspiration 🔺.. 166

commercial 4

Introduction... 172
INVESCO Field at Mile High... 174
Watermark Luxury Residences... 184
Arraya Tower.. 198
1999 Broadway.. 208
Bell Tower.. 218
Dubai Towers.. 222
Wearable Art 🦋.. 226

community **5**

Introduction..234
Semper Fidelis Memorial Park and Chapel...............................236
The Chapel at Cherry Hills Community Church...........................240
Mile Hi Church...244
Music + Dance + Architecture 🕺...................................248

civic +
government **6**

Introduction..254
Clark County Government Center...256
Jefferson County Government Center....................................268
Jefferson County Human Services Building..............................276
Oakland Administration Buildings..280
Sacramento City Hall..292
Natural Resources Building..298
San Joaquin County Administration Building............................302
California Department of Education Headquarters.......................308
Light + Movement ☼...312

courts **7**

Introduction..318
Ralph L Carr Colorado Judicial Center..................................320
Al Farwania and Al Jahra Court Complexes.............................326
Norfolk Consolidated Courts Complex...................................330
Stone + Dignity ⬢..334

education +
laboratories **8**

Introduction..340
University of Colorado Denver Research 1 and Research 2..............342
Sanford Consortium for Regenerative Medicine.........................348
David E. Skaggs Federal Building | NOAA Headquarters................352
University of Colorado Mathematics Building and Gemmill Engineering Library..............356
University of California | Irvine Gateway Humanities Building..........360
Breakthrough Thoughts + Innovation 🗿.............................364

Credits...368

to begin

Buildings and plans may fill this book, but they do not define its meaning. People do. Both the hundreds who have passionately pursued design at Fentress Architects since the studio's beginnings in 1980, and the millions who bring these buildings to life by using them every day.

"Design for people" sums up the studio's philosophy. It's the embodiment of the principles they follow, Fentress' Touchstones of Design. It's why they do what they do, why these pages include not only the story of 39 projects but the cultural influences that inform our lives. No one works in a vacuum, especially not an architect who believes in immersing himself and his studio in the culture of a community.

Public Architecture: The Art Inside is the thirteenth book written about Curtis Fentress or his studio. It is the first general portfolio book in a decade. During that period, the studio has become local in four cities, and its commissions have included landmark buildings on three continents.

Public architecture remains their focus, and not because it involves complex buildings such as airports, museums, convention centers, government centers, and courthouses. These projects are important because all are places where people gather, whether it's to embark on a trip to new and exciting places, learn and play, connect with elected leaders, or seek justice. People are the beating heart of these projects.

Creating a book is like building a building. It takes a team, and I would like to thank those who made this book real.

First, naturally, is a studio that over the years has been energized by talented and committed people who pursue innovative and sustainable designs that last. This book includes the studio's new projects, designs in process, and those from an earlier time. These buildings seek that elusive balance between art and function, and all reflect the enthusiasm of a studio that understands the connections forged in place, people and pride. Without the determination and talent of the people in the studio, these pages would be blank.

As this book is published, Fentress caps off its thirtieth anniversary. The constant reminder of the importance of people in our built environment is the foundation of everything the studio does, now and in the future.

Many people have become crucial to the creation of this book, starting with CEO Agatha Kessler, who had the vision to explore cultural and scientific influences on architecture and design. These essays open a door to the world of art, music, fashion and innovation, and the impact of these disciplines on Fentress' design and architecture. Throughout the book, I was greatly assisted by photographer and photo archivist Jason A. Knowles and designer Edward W. Huang, with design and technical assistance from Matt Aune. Members of the communications and marketing teams were invaluable in their help. Noted architectural writer John Morris Dixon and designer/educator Michael McCoy added clarity to the meaning of public architecture, while writer and filmmaker Andrew Cohen and publisher Gordon Goff provided layering to the cultural aspect of the book.

Finally, my thanks go to Curt Fentress for his help on this project and his generosity with his time. He knows these buildings inside and out, remembers every plan, every photo, and every moment of the design and execution of 30-plus years worth of architectural achievement. He is at the heart of this book, though he would never say that. To him, I believe, the buildings, the people who made them, and the people who use them are what count. As one of the millions of people who experiences his work every day, and after countless interviews, I have a new admiration for Curt's talent and his commitment to creating inspired design for people.

Again, thank you.

Mary Voelz Chandler
November 2010

biography

Curtis Fentress came to Denver in the late 1970s to work on an office tower for the fledgling New York-based firm of Kohn Pedersen Fox. He had joined KPF after five years with I.M. Pei, where Fentress continued his pursuit of large-scale public projects while injecting humanism into civic buildings.

In 1980, Fentress was named "Young Professional of the Year" by *Building Design and Construction* magazine. He couldn't leave Denver, lured by the natural beauty of the city and state, the incredible sunshine, and the friendliness of the people. So he founded a studio and called Denver his home.

It was a long and fulfilling journey for a man born in a log cabin on a tobacco farm in North Carolina. As a child, Fentress discovered drawing, and his love of that and encouragement from teachers led him into drafting and architecture. He attended the College of Design at North Carolina State University, where he graduated with honors. There, he won an AIA-FAIA Fellowship, a Graham Foundation Fellowship, and the Alpha Rho Chi Medal, the highest honor given a designer by an architecture school.

Fentress' belief in Denver's opportunities and optimism soon paid off with commissions that mixed challenge and reward, from key office towers such as 1999 Broadway to renovations of notable buildings. When city officials asked him to design the passenger terminal at Denver International Airport, the Fentress studio was propelled into the national spotlight and the international realm.

Through forty years as an architect – thirty leading his own studio – Fentress' heart has stayed true to public architecture, the airports, museums, convention centers, civic centers, government complexes and educational and scientific facilities that require a commitment to the people who commission, pay for, work in and live with these singular buildings. Each design is inspired by the community it serves, by the context and culture rooted in place, pride and people.

The studio's pioneering belief in innovative and sustainable design extends to thorough process. This unspoken promise with the community strives to unify all parties in a focused and respectful search for a one-of-a-kind building that will last and reflect conscientious environmental stewardship.

These principles, embodied in the eight Touchstones of Design, represent a commitment to the civic arena, signaled by the American Institute of Architects' decision in 2010 to honor Fentress with the Thomas Jefferson Award, the highest accolade given to those who devote their practice to the field of public architecture. This award is among more than 330 the studio has garnered for its dedication to design that balances art and function in a meaningful and enduring way. It is a point of equilibrium that considers the practical and the inspirational, the careful and the joyful, in order to replicate the impact of civic buildings on people.

"Some architects have a preconceived notion of what a building should be – they design from the outside like the building is a piece of sculpture. I prefer to patiently search through extensive discovery until I find a seam somewhere, crack it open and discover the art inside," says Fentress, FAIA, RIBA, principal-in-charge of design.

Curtis Fentress
on architecture

to begin at the beginning: "why architecture?"

In high school, I read lots of books on architects, Thomas Jefferson, Bruce Goff, Frank Lloyd Wright and others. I wrote a high school English paper on Wright. I took art and drafting classes, and I wasn't the best or anything, but I had a great passion for art and drafting. Both my art teacher and drafting teacher were saying, "Have you ever thought of being an architect or engineer?" I pretty much finished everything in the drafting class that was in the book, and the teacher didn't know what to do with me because I went through it so quickly. That teacher got me an after-school job drafting for a civil engineering company, where I drafted plot plans for topographic information. My first year in college, I was in engineering school.

how did you go from engineering to architecture?

I used to spend Saturdays in the College of Design library. My dorm was right across the street from the school on a quad of dorms. I managed one of them, as part of my work-study program, and got a free place to stay. I'd get up early on Saturdays and spend a good portion of the day just looking at books on architecture. They had fabulous books on all the great architects: Alvar Aalto, Le Corbusier, Frank Lloyd Wright, and all the architects in California doing Modernist houses in L.A. Anytime I didn't have anything to do between classes, I'd go to the library.

Saarinen was the one I was most interested in. I liked the fact that all his buildings were different. And they were more about what he saw as a problem-solver. I had a professor who had worked for him, had built some of the models for TWA. I had an interest in that firm and always have had, and the way that the firm evolved. When Saarinen passed away, Kevin Roche and John Dinkeloo stepped in and took over the firm. My old partner Jim Bradburn used to work for them, too. That's how we got together and why we worked so well together for so many years.

what was it like working in I.M. Pei's office?

In Pei's office I worked a lot for Jim Freed, Harry Cobb and on a couple of projects with Mr. Pei. I had personal experience with all three, but mostly with Jim. I worked on a number of projects that were never built. It was first-hand experience of working with these great mentors and masters. It was terrific. I worked 90 hours a week, that kind of thing. Those guys worked on the weekends and after hours. So there was a lot of opportunity to work directly with the three of them and see how they approached things and made decisions. During this period of time, I studied urban design at Columbia, but when people ask where I went to graduate school, I always say at I.M. Pei.

Curtis Fentress
on architecture

why did you leave?

I had worked there for five years, then was recruited by the newly formed Kohn Pedersen Fox. There were so many good people stacked up in Pei's office. The pyramid was pretty solid. To rise up the pyramid was a lifetime challenge. Leaving Pei for KPF was one of the most difficult decisions I've ever made. It was a wonderful place to work. They treated me really well. And when I left, they said you can always come back. I had a lot of good friends, still do, from that office. At KPF, things happened. They had a tremendous run of work in New York. It was tough work. It was development office buildings.

All of a sudden, ABC, the broadcasting company, took off and ordered a bunch of buildings. Then there were the telephone company jobs. I worked for that firm for three years. I designed a couple of projects in Denver that were not as attractive to the partners as other work. They preferred other places, not to go to Denver. I took something that seems like a lemon and made lemonade out of it. That's how I got to Denver.

Architecturally, it gave me the chance to break free from the grid. With Pei, I had spent five years as a slave to the grid. He built gorgeous, solid buildings. Very sculptural. But after five years I was interested in doing things that were not hung up on the grid. The whole shape and form of the Amoco Building, for Kohn Pedersen Fox, responded to the context. Drawing a line down 17th Street as it defined Broadway generated a line that made a hexagon shape. Putting in the atrium, creating a place for people – I had some freedom on that design.

the Touchstones of Design involve design principles, but they are not stylistically strict. how did you avoid the "isms" over the years, like Postmodernism, and not get locked into one style?

To me, it's about the context, the site, the culture, and finding the natural order, allowing what happens inside the building to inform how we shape the building. It's about why we're building it, and why the client needs it. That's part of the evolution of the Touchstones. To me, initially, it's the context, the function, and then celebrating the entry. Gradually, it evolved into eight Touchstones that guide my design.

one comment I've heard about forward-looking buildings keys off Robert Frost's poem about good fences, but with a twist: that really good buildings don't make good neighbors. they can be too flamboyant, too much in the foreground to be respectful of their context. do you think architects are pulling back in terms of up-front design?

What makes a city is its landmarks. We migrate to landmarks. They are what make a city one of a kind. But there may be times when iconic buildings may not be good neighbors.

When I went to Pei's office, one of the associates there said, "You can design a building and have all the parts made. That's what we do. Or you can design a building, and pick all the parts from a catalog. That's what they do at XYZ firms." It's not building with a kit of parts. It also has to do with the integrity of the building.

I heard a story about Renzo Piano. A client asked him to take money out of the budget. So Piano designed a building out of cinderblock, instead of granite. It's the cheapest thing you can use. He presented it. And he said all the architectural stuff about how wonderful it is and how poetic it is. At the end of the meeting, the man in charge said, "I'd feel really cheap if you put that on my building. Everybody is going to think I'm really cheap." The granite came back.

what's the state of architecture today?

Everyone is at the top of their game right now, in education, computer modeling, and technology. We are all very highly skilled artists and technicians at this point. As we finish this period, there may be a little bit of a sway, because the pendulum has swung a little too far in terms of the iconic nature of buildings. Everyone wanted an iconic building. That word has been overused a lot. The next period will be much more pragmatic, straightforward and, in a way, more responsible.

after 40 years, where are you as an architect?

I'm as much a student of architecture now as I was 40 years ago. The difference is, now I know what I don't know. When I say architecture is a patient search, I mean for a lifetime. It's a lifetime of studying and hard work. People ask, "What do you do for vacation? What do you do in your spare time?" I go look at buildings. When I travel, I visit buildings. I am a perpetual student of architecture. Every building is part of a unique experience. I guess that's why I have such a great appreciation of what Saarinen was doing. It's a labor of love.

design and function meet in public

John Morris Dixon FAIA

John Morris Dixon, an architecture graduate of MIT, was chief editor of *Progressive Architecture* magazine from 1972 to 1996. More recently, he has written for such magazines as *Architect, Architecture, Architectural Record*, and *Competitions*. Dixon has contributed essays to numerous books, including *Civic Builders* by Curtis Fentress, and is the author of *The World Bank*. He is now writing a book tracing the evolution of Modern architecture from the 1950s to the present. A Fellow of the American Institute of Architects, Dixon is a past chair of the AIA Committee on Design, on which he remains active.

Public architecture must always appeal to a broad range of users. And because works of public architecture serve many first-time or infrequent visitors, it's especially important for entrances and interior paths to be apparent. What's more, public architecture often comes to represent the institution and/or the place where it is built, thus becoming symbolic – if only by displaying such abstract qualities as caution or daring, detachment or community engagement.

Through much of history, there has been a strong tendency for any structures serving a large public to be monumental – large in scale, symmetrical, often fitting a variety of internal functions into a unified volume. The Modernists of the early twentieth century, on the other hand, scorned monumentality and focused on abstract composition, rather than symbolic unity. Their buildings sometimes appeared bland or utilitarian. By mid-century, monumentality and symbolism were returning, but the resulting architecture, unrestrained by earlier conventions, often turned out to look awkwardly massive. The decades since the 1950s have seen diverse efforts to develop appropriate imagery for structures that serve the public.

Fentress has been privileged to create public architecture of many kinds: government buildings, airport terminals, museums, and convention centers among them. Its history of public architecture commissions reflects the fact that these are more likely than private projects to be awarded through design competitions. Since its launch in 1980, with a practice at the time dominated by office buildings, the studio has built its portfolio of public structures in large part by entering design competitions – and winning remarkably many.

Unlike most comparably established firms, Fentress continues to enter design competitions, recently four or five of them a year. Fentress prefers two-stage competitions, where the finalist firms are able to refine initial concepts through deeper study of the project's program and circumstances. He observes that even a failed entry yields benefits for participants in terms of experience and knowledge applicable to subsequent work.

As Fentress points out, clients who initiate design competitions are those who want "stronger" design, "something of an icon." In its public structures, Fentress has trod a careful line between boldness and prudence, exhibiting symbolism and geographical allusions that are sometimes quite literal, sometimes subtle. As he notes, the memorable silhouette of the Denver International Airport terminal can be construed as an allusion to the Rocky Mountains, visible nearby, or to tepees indigenous to the surrounding High Plains. Yet its sculptural roof is at the same time a functional and technologically advanced means to span a large volume, as effective for the luminous interior it provides as for its exterior imagery.

The firm's design for a new terminal at Los Angeles International Airport will produce a profile recalling the wavelets of the Pacific, which is just off the end of its runways. This imagery, as well, springs from a functional system for spanning the interiors and providing them with ample daylight. Other features of this design are structural arches that echo those of the airport's 1961 central Theme Building, reintegrating what had become a forlornly isolated icon, unrelated to the facilities clustered around it.

In some of its work in the mountain states and the Southwest, the studio has generated forms that allude fairly literally either to geographic features, as in the National Museum of Wildlife Art, or to local design traditions, as in the Santa Fe Community Convention Center. For a public bus station in Tucson, the firm incorporated the unself-conscious architectural motifs of a Southwestern downtown – along with recycled brick from nearby buildings.

architecture

At the National Museum of the Marine Corps, the structure had to represent the modern Corps while recognizing its special sense of historical mission. The building's central architectural feature originated as an abstraction of the iconic photo of the flag-raising at Iwo Jima: a series of structural struts raise a central shaft at an angle, as if straining to make it vertical. But whatever the symbolic nature of its public architecture, Fentress gives equal attention to its comprehensibility, to the need for members of the public to find their way into and about the interior. In terms of indicating entry points, the Pasadena Convention Center presents a special case where equivalent prominence had to be given to three different entrances: doorways to the auditorium in the preexisting central building and those to the two flanking wings, each with an equally important function.

Airports present a special challenge, since movement through them needs to be narrowly yet clearly prescribed. Fentress often uses daylight ahead to draw users toward their destinations. The paths of arriving passengers demand even more attention, since strict functionalism typically yields a sequence of low, viewless spaces. Fentress cites the example of the Incheon International Airport terminal, where arriving passengers proceed through a daylighted two-story space featuring a waterfall and a Zen garden setting. At the studio's new terminal at Los Angeles International Airport, arriving passengers will proceed through glazed passages a level above the departure hall, offering them welcoming views of city and mountains.

In the current economic climate, Fentress expects clients to continue looking for structures that are both functional and exciting. But those paying the bills — whether voters or board members — have become more bottom line-oriented. They'll be more concerned not only with costs, but with avoiding the appearance of extravagance. The striving for the "Bilbao effect," the search for an avant-garde landmark to put the locality on the map, is now largely on hold. In this environment, the Fentress strategy of deriving architectural forms from local circumstances — with no preconceived brand of imagery — promises to yield designs that truly serve the public.

Curtis Fentress &
the architecture

Michael McCoy

Michael McCoy writes and lectures widely on the intersection of technology and design. The recipient of over 200 awards for his designs for Knoll, Philips, Steelcase and Humanscale, McCoy's work has been exhibited at museums worldwide. After 23 years as co-chairs of the Design Department at Cranbrook Academy, he and his wife, Katherine, have written *Cranbrook Design: The New Discourse*. They are directors of High Ground Design Workshops and former faculty at the Institute of Design at the Illinois Institute of Technology (IIT) in Chicago. They received the Smithsonian Institution's first Design Minds National Design Award for "affecting a paradigm shift in the design profession."

As you approach Denver from the air, you first see Denver International Airport on the horizon from many miles away. It appears to be a small mountain range rising from the plains or a village of tepees. As you land, you view it as a luminous tent-like structure with varied peaks and valleys, and it beckons to you to enter it and explore. As you emerge from the train into the enormous fabric-covered space supported by huge angled columns and a view of the mountains, you receive an expansive welcome to Denver. It's a great first impression.

Driving into the city you pass INVESCO Field (home of the Denver Broncos) with undulating lines that suggest the fluidity of athletes and the public celebration of games.

Entering downtown, you pass under the dramatically angled cantilevered roof of the Colorado Convention Center and into downtown. Walking from the city into the building, through its spectacular glass entrance wall, you are drawn through the grand central hall to the theater at the far end by the compelling views of the mountains.

In this journey you have just experienced Curt Fentress' vision of public architecture and the city.

Cities need iconic welcoming gateways to announce the character and spirit of the community, and engaging architectural experiences to draw people downtown. Curt has provided both for Denver.

His Denver International Airport has become the symbol for Denver and the Rocky Mountain region, just as the St. Louis Gateway Arch became the symbol for that city and the Eiffel Tower became the symbol for Paris.

Public architecture should be optimistic, expansive, welcoming and permeable to the community and visitors. Fentress achieves this through transparency, translucency, uplift, and flow. There seems to be an upward force in much of his work. Even in his most high-tech buildings, nature is evoked through curvilinear geometry, natural materials, and wave forms. His spaces are airy and light.

The lyrical forms of INVESCO Field invoke and even invite "the wave" motion of sports fans. Crowds move through his spaces with ease. The parking garage of the Colorado Convention Center, with its curvaceous walls of perforated metal, is arguably the planet's best-looking garage.

All of those compositional elements contribute to the sense of flow in the spaces. You are enticed to move through the space because you want to discover more. Discovery is possible because of the many variations on the architectural theme that promise surprise. To know one part of a Fentress building is not to know all parts, unlike systems architecture, in which you get the idea immediately and there is no further discovery.

# of experience

Fentress' architectural forms often imply imagery, consciously and unconsciously. People view the Denver airport as representing the mountain peaks to the west, tepees on the prairie, or the covered wagons of the pioneers, the latter two variations on tensile fabric structures.

In fact, the tensile-strength Teflon®-coated fiberglass roof is one of the most practical solutions for covering a large public space, as it provides natural daylighting and sheds snow efficiently. It's a very "green" solution that consumes far less energy for daytime lighting. Curt manages to design energy-efficient buildings that are uplifting rather than punitive and stingy.

That brings up another aspect of Fentress' approach – practicality in creating well-designed, visionary projects that are completed on time and on budget. That is why he wins so many large public projects around the world that actually get built.

Because he does not have a repetitive iconography that is duplicated for every project regardless of the locale, culture and specific program, it's possible to enjoy a Fentress building without even knowing that he designed it. That happened to me at Incheon International Airport in Seoul, South Korea, which is spectacular and a great experience. It was an impressive and sophisticated welcome to the city, expressing to me that Seoul was becoming one of the innovation centers for the world. It was only later that I learned that Curt had designed it.

His new design for LAX, with its arched bridges connecting new wave-form concourses with views of the mountains and city, will finally give Los Angeles a gateway airport worthy of the city.

One important aspect to designing a building that flows naturally is the idea of transparency, as opposed to opacity. At the Denver airport you arrive and check in, and then emerge on a mezzanine looking down on the main hall. From there you can immediately sense where to go for dining, purchasing a book, or entering security (and how long the lines are). You can create a mental map of the dynamic of the space at a glance. No long maze of tunnels and cryptic signs; it's all laid out in front of you. And there is a sense of universal order that is rare in this day and age in seeing everything and everyone moving along on their journey.

Public architecture is a fundamentally positive act, and it should not be approached in a cynical or defensive way. Curt's positive democratic attitude is very evident in his work. He seems to expect the best from everyone in his spaces, and they respond to that in kind.

Curt's process is one of curiosity and observation about the circumstances and context and situation. He likes to take notes and sketch, all the time and everywhere, including on the backs of envelopes. The sketches capture essences and lead to plans and form concepts.

The Fentress design language and iconography is not presupposed but evolves after a careful study of the situation. The building does not appear to be a packaged solution inserted into the landscape, but rather the result of a contemplative process of thinking about the site, the community and the program. The form language, the plan, the composition, the materials and the technology are all custom-designed for the particular scenario, one client at a time.

Curt's message through his work is: let's celebrate our landscape, our community, our history, our culture and our people through our public spaces. Ultimately, public architecture is about people.

1

AIRPORTS

DENVER INTERNATIONAL AIRPORT
INCHEON INTERNATIONAL AIRPORT
LOS ANGELES INTERNATIONAL AIRPORT
SAN JOSE INTERNATIONAL AIRPORT
SEATTLE-TACOMA INTERNATIONAL AIRPORT
RALEIGH-DURHAM INTERNATIONAL AIRPORT

AIRPORTS

The romance of air travel has been declared dead more than once, but it's wise to consider that judgment premature.

Though many of the world's airports suffer from confusing navigation and dreary interiors, a movement began in the 1990s to design airports that draw from the imagery of flight and recall the grandeur of buildings devoted to transportation.

This awakening began near the center of the United States — Denver — at a studio that set a new standard facing a tough deadline.

With the design of Denver International Airport's (DIA) terminal and Great Hall, the Fentress studio raised the bar for the way in which airports can satisfy basic needs such as functionality, flexibility and sustainability. Beauty, however, is not a luxury here; it is a necessity, with a strong influence on how people feel, think and act. The circulation is intuitive, using organizational strategies that are easy to understand and sensible, while saving money and allowing airports and airlines to adapt quickly to new technology and security measures.

An airport must not be a "people processor"; thus, the human experience is a primary consideration in every Fentress design. The concept of humanism flows through these gigantic public spaces,

keyed to people and to passenger comforts and conveniences, through the use of abundant daylight and references to a region's context and culture. Ultimately, the success of an airport rests on the way it allows travelers to know where they are going, offers spaces to relax and reflect, and provides amenities that soften some of the strains of travel.

Fentress' work on DIA, the first greenfield airport to be built in the United States in decades, propelled the studio into a leadership position in the realm of airport design. The concept of "changing the paradigm" has almost become a cliché. At Denver's airport, however, it is a simple fact: combining technological innovation, savvy cost-saving techniques, and the goal of well-being, helped put DIA on the map, and open international doors.

Then comes Incheon International Airport, a passenger-pleasing development that operates on land reclaimed from nearby islands. An open, airy design accommodates more than upscale amenities and services. Incheon incorporates cultural cues as a matter of course, not something tacked on or turned into a cartoon version of an amusement park. Architectural elements pulled from Korea's heritage, gardens that speak to the Korean soul, and attractions that celebrate Korea's culture are integral to the plan. No wonder more than 8.6 million travelers have voted Incheon best airport over the past five years.

From two vast greenfield airports, Fentress turned to the challenge of facilities that need to maintain smooth daily operations within tight boundaries. At Seattle-Tacoma International Airport, the goal was to give the place a heart, a marketplace that showed respect to the cities' thriving and historic public markets.

The design for Raleigh-Durham International Airport reflects the dichotomy of North Carolina's tradition of craft and its forward-thinking, high-tech educational facilities and industries. Meanwhile, San Jose International Airport bears witness to that city's key role in Silicon Valley, birthplace of the world's new technologies and new ways of living and learning.

For Los Angeles International Airport, which has long belied its city's reputation for glamour and sun-drenched environment, the Fentress design calls for making sense of years of add-on facilities, providing a rational and instinctive travel experience, giving travelers a taste of the natural splendor that surrounds LA, that is LA.

Over and over, Fentress continues to demonstrate that beauty and practicality travel well.

Project **Passenger Terminal Complex**
Location **Denver, Colorado**
Client **City and County of Denver**
Year **1995**

Curtis Fentress "Yes, we created a metaphor for the mountains, and, yes, we related it to place. We had the idea of embracing the light, which was very special at this location. But there was also a lot of problem-solving at DIA. We used technology to shorten the schedule, so that being more thoughtful in the design saved tons of steel, tons of concrete, and months of construction. In a sense, we flipped the building upside down to make it work."

1

DEN

Curtis Fentress began thinking about airports long before he became an architect. He was drawing airplanes as a child, and building structures while at play in the sandbox. In architecture school, his fascination with travel led him to devote his graduate project to airport design, an exploration that now shows how drastically our relationship with airports has evolved.

Fentress based his thesis on the quaint concept of "kiss and fly," a reference to the days when airports were smaller, surface parking was adequate, a short sprint would land travelers at the door of the airplane, and the word "hub" was usually connected to the word "cap."

But then travel expanded dramatically, both domestic and global, requiring more parking. Airlines developed the hub-and-spoke organization for efficiency. Airports grew, and grew, in the process losing aesthetic impact and the sense that travel was both easy and a pleasure. Passenger comfort was second to protocol.

When the City and County of Denver asked Fentress and team to prepare a conceptual design for a terminal building for its new airport, they were able to take outdated theory and put it into forward-thinking practice. When DIA landed in the Fentress studio, the project was behind schedule, busting its budget, and sporting an unimpressive design. The city wanted a symbol as much as a gateway, a building as visually memorable as it was functional. The project was seen as an economic driver: a rare gift of 53 square miles of open land ripe for commercial and residential development in an early concept of an airport city.

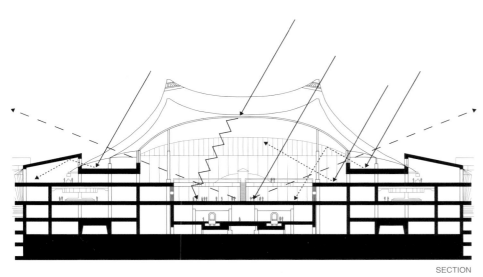

The impact of different types of light on the Terminal's Great Hall is demonstrated in the section differentiating paths of direct, diffused and refracted light produced by the tent-like roof.

SECTION

The Rocky Mountains help define Denver both geographically and spiritually, and serve as an inspiration for the "peaks" at Denver International Airport. They are shown in sketches by Curtis Fentress and, in finished form, silhouetted against the brilliant clouds.

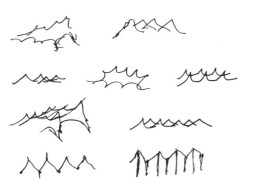

Fentress and team worked on a punishing deadline of three weeks. They quickly determined that the answer to the city's problems was to flip the terminal upside down, putting mechanical systems in the basement and designing a tensile-strength, Teflon®-coated roof that was easy to assemble, durable and like nothing Denver had ever seen. And because it did not require a massive frame or a heavy foundation, it massaged the budget by requiring less steel, concrete and time.

"We were able to take out 300 tons of steel and 200,000 linear feet of concrete foundation walls," says Curtis Fentress, noting that the bid was $40 million under budget, saving the city $115 million. "We designed it so the roof was made in a factory and brought out, unrolled, and put up, very quickly." Once the roof was on, interior construction could continue to save the project time, for a terminal and Great Hall that focus on intuitive circulation and abundant daylight.

If the overall design found favor, the material caused some concerns among city officials, who feared the fabric roof might not hold up under Colorado's occasional snow dump, especially on the plains east of Denver. But Fentress' then-partner James Bradburn had visited structures with fabric roofs in Canada to learn about their performance. The main problem there: seagulls dropping fish bones on the tent-like structures.

The resulting DIA terminal building demonstrates an architectural approach that stresses expression, letting the snowy white roof serve as metaphor for place, culture and imagination. Fentress designed expansive glass curtain walls that brought in the mood-elevating Colorado sun, adding sustainability to the building and setting the stage for a greener DIA. The roof material allows 10 percent of visible light to pass through the fabric for daylighting, diminishing the need for indoor lighting during the day; the bright, white roof reflects 90 percent of the high-altitude ultraviolet rays. DIA later installed a "solar farm" with 9,000 panels producing 3.5 million kilowatts of electricity.

SOUTH ELEVATION

SECTION

CROSS-SECTION

In section and elevation, the fabric roof ties together aspects of the airport terminal, adding loft and airiness to a vast public space.

Canopies at the entries of the Terminal reflect the outline of the roof structure and share the same Teflon®-coated, tensile-strength fabric.

Just as Eero Saarinen's design for Terminal 5 at John F. Kennedy International Airport relied on sculptural form to explore the metaphor of flight, "our structure at DIA is expressive. It's emblematic, this fine edge of working with structure, working with form, and working with the building to express something that is not too literal."

*

Denver International Airport in 2009 served 50.2 million passengers, over its capacity of 50 million. There are 95 gates, which, if modified, can accommodate the A-380 Airbus.

The design for Denver International Airport propelled the firm into the national spotlight and the international realm.

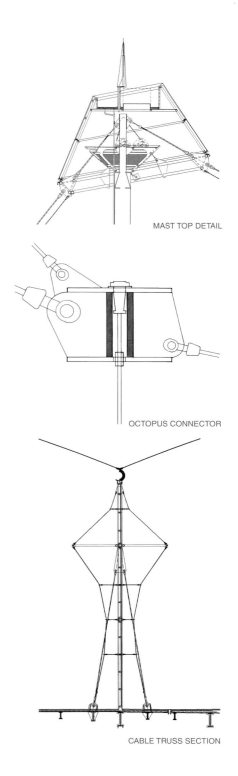

MAST TOP DETAIL

OCTOPUS CONNECTOR

CABLE TRUSS SECTION

The roof fabric weighs about two pounds per square foot, with the stitched sections supported and stabilized by a cable truss and anchor system.

ART, INSIDE AND OUT

The land that became Denver International Airport is emblematic of Colorado's Eastern Plains. This expansive vista helped inspire development of a public art program for DIA that focused on the themes of land, cultural context, and transportation. Planning for what became more than $7.5 million in artwork at DIA began in the late 1980s, and grew into the largest airport public art program at the time aiming to integrate art into architecture. Artist-designed terrazzo floors hailed Native American directional colors, while 5,280 backlit propellers – a nod to Denver's altitude – swirled in a tunnel for the train carrying travelers from concourses to terminal.

The piece that carries the most drama also took the longest to complete: fifteen years after the airport art program hired sculptor Luis Jimenez to create a 32-foot rearing mustang with a blue fiberglass skin, *Mustang / Mesteño* was installed near the airport terminal. In the process of being fabricated, a section of the work came loose and fell on Jimenez, killing the artist. But *Mustang*, like other works by Jimenez, is a vital piece, with flashing red eyes and a proud stance that greets travelers whether they are arriving at or leaving the airport. In this protracted long process, Denver residents have formed a love-hate relationship with the *Mustang*, adding to the long history of debate on art.

Lighting in the Terminal interior benefits from a gleaming granite floor (left). Public art by Patty Ortiz doubles as a wayfinding device (top left). Smart lighting and an expansive white ceiling work together to brighten the Terminal.

(Following spread) Like a mirage on a spring-green prairie, the Terminal roof appears to nestle against the Rocky Mountains, evoking the image of Native American tepees.

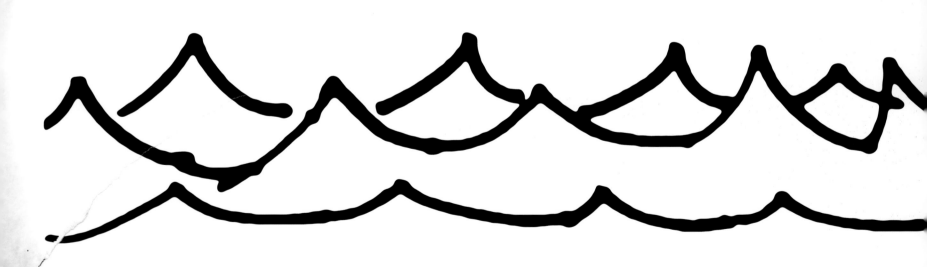

Project **Passenger Terminal Complex**
Location **Seoul, South Korea**
Client **Korean Airport Construction Authority**
Owner **Incheon International Airport Corporation**
Year **2001**

Curtis Fentress "I was looking for that essence of line. Is there a line that is distinctly Korean? I thought about the way traditional Korean homes are built. The carpenter puts in two pins, and then stretches a rope between them, which forms a catenary. That curve speaks to the Korean form."

2

ICN

A thriving economy and tourism business boosted by the 1988 Summer Olympics in Seoul led South Korean officials to consider how to address the capital city's airport. The existing Gimpo Airport couldn't handle the influx of visitors, especially as the nation was being transformed into a democracy and an increasingly attractive destination. This led officials to begin plans to construct a new airport to serve the growing number of international flights. Seoul was determined to become a major gateway for travel to Asia.

For Fentress Architects, which in 1992 won the international competition to design the passenger terminal complex, decoding Incheon meant using cultural cues, contextual references and humanizing elements to add warmth and ease of navigation to a huge, important space.

It was all about achieving a sense of place.

But first a place had to be built: Incheon sits on a 50-square-mile site created between two island mountains, where dikes and infill from the mountains produced the needed land for both an airport and an airport city. The latter is intended for more than residents drawn to new space; an airport city is a trade nexus, linking ocean, land and sky in commerce. Fentress' experience in working on Denver International Airport, another massive from-scratch greenfield airport, helped gain entrée to the competition. But it was immersion and research into the nation's aesthetics that informed the design and won the commission.

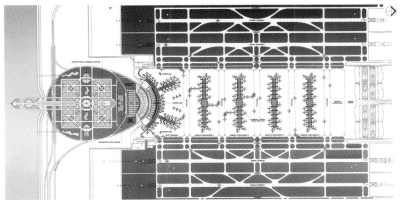

MASTER PLAN

Sinuous lines set the tone for the curbside bridge between the Terminal and the Transportation Center (top). The site plan illustrates the Incheon International Airport master plan (at left), while an aerial photograph shows the Terminal under construction.

Once the firm was shortlisted, Curtis Fentress spent several weeks in South Korea searching for not just civic information, but also a sense of Korea's cultural and architectural heritage. He toured museums and historic sites, and sampled the native foods. He found that Koreans traditionally had used heated floors in their homes, among the sustainable ideas they employed. As tools improved, so did the durability of building materials, allowing the shift from thatch, to wood, to stone. Patterns and geometries found only in Korean design and crafts have survived for millennia.

Allusions to Korean line and crafts, as well as the inclusion of Korean landscaping concepts, give Incheon a human scale. Korean cultural and performance experiences also are part of the mix, as are high-end shops and restaurants. A high-tech ceiling superstructure references the traditional Korean pagoda geometry, while panoramic curved curtain walls allow natural light to not just flood the terminal but also nurture nature, and man. Gardens are designed with an eye toward Koreans' paradoxical preference for both interaction and contemplation.

"We introduced the gardens into the central spaces to calm the senses," says Thom Walsh, principal.

Yet being literal was neither possible nor desirable in a massive complex that needed to remain flexible for the ever-changing airline industry. Capturing the essence was essential, and the only honest way to design a modern, high-tech airport that still remained rooted in its home soil.

And that came back full circle, to the line.

"The section of the building with that catenary sweep, the curve, and the columns that went up with cables – that kept the profile of the Korean home," says Fentress. "The floors we treated conceptually – very simple and straightforward in pattern. The result is Korean, but in an abstract way."

*

In 2009, Incheon International Airport served 28.5 million passengers, with a capacity of 44 million. There are 74 gates. Incheon can accommodate service for stage 4 aircraft including the A380.

A rare view of Incheon's Terminal (left) from airside shows the sweep of the structure and its generous use of glass.

Line and landscape mark the design inspiration for Incheon, as demonstrated (right) by the type of catenary curve found in traditional Korean architecture and the love of peaceful garden settings.

The "curbside wedge" of the Terminal relies on a strong roofline gesture and cornice (facing page). Circulation at Incheon is made simple and intuitive through the inclusion of moving sidewalks, escalators and an easy-to-read multilingual wayfinding system.

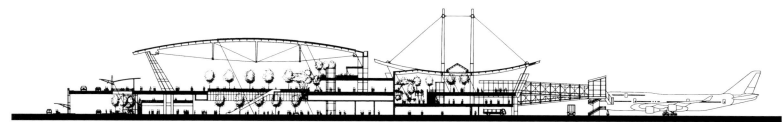

MAIN TERMINAL SECTION

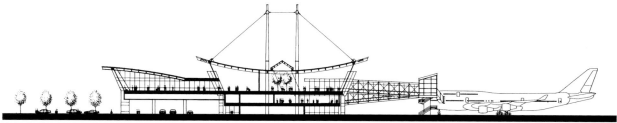

DOMESTIC CONCOURSE SECTION

Incheon's curbside area is marked by graceful curves and an intuitive traffic flow (above). The upper-level walkway combines the transparency of a glass floor and the contextual warmth of wooden columns (left).

Clerestories and glass walls bring natural light into the Terminal interior, where stands of trees and easily maintained light fixtures add a natural touch (following spread).

RECLAIMED LAND FOR AIRPORTS

Incheon International Airport began as an idea without a home. To build it, dikes were constructed to keep out the sea water, and earth was dug out from the mountains on two adjacent islands, then removed to use as fill between the two small land masses. In this way, officials created a 50-square-mile platform for an airport and airport city. Apparently, at low tide, a person could walk from island to island on land that rested solidly on granite. Still, the reclamation effort was an expensive proposition, costing more than $10 billion. Incheon, which opened in 2001, is not the first airport to be built on an artificial island or reclaimed land. Kansai opened in 1994, and Hong Kong's Chek Lap Kok International Airport began operations in 1998, on land predominantly reclaimed from two neighboring islands, one of which loaned its name to the airport.

Project **Bradley West International Passenger Terminal Modernization + LAX Master Plan**
Location **Los Angeles, California**
Client **Los Angeles World Airports**
Year **Phase 1: 2012**

Los Angeles Mayor Antonio Villaraigosa "The Fentress design for LAX is spectacular, embodying the character of Los Angeles and creating a remarkable sense of place. It is unmistakably LA."

3

LAX

Los Angeles is where the stars come out to play, where the sun always shines, and where millions of people have migrated over the years to create a vibrant and diverse mix of cultures and communities. They've chased the California dream.

But the city's gateway to the world – LAX – has become more of a nightmare. Its nine terminals lack connections, and the circulation needs a sense of flow. Amenities such as food and retail are bare-bones. International passengers are greeted by a dark, forbidding corridor leading to security and customs, hardly the kind of welcome a city built on beauty and illusion should give people pumping millions of dollars into the regional economy. The place is so behind the times that some travelers have chosen to use other West Coast airports as their entry point into the United States. What should be L.A.'s powerful economic driver and image-maker has proved to be just the opposite.

So for Fentress, winning the commission to masterplan and modernize the airport was an opportunity to put years of airport expertise into play, to make sense of how the airport worked, to bring light and comfort to travelers, and to transplant the personality of Southern California into its nominal front door.

Fentress began the process of untangling circulation and injecting life into LAX by talking to residents, city officials and travelers about what Los Angeles means to them. These visioning sessions produced words and phrases that speak L.A.'s language: culture, celebrity, openness, diversity, creativity, trendsetting and all manner of descriptions of the area's natural beauty.

MASTER PLAN

The master plan (left) shows the unifying aspects of the Terminal expansion and planned pedestrian bridge depicted above. A sky train is planned to connect the Terminal, car rental facilities, and LA's public transportation system.

But as Fentress listened, it became clear that the beach, ocean and sun – were the reasons people continue to come.

"When you sit and talk to people, they all brought up the beach and the boardwalk, the waves and the sun," says Curtis Fentress.

That unifying theme generated a coherent design vocabulary for the Bradley West Project, the first major improvement at LAX since the construction of the Bradley Terminal for the Summer Olympics more than 25 years ago. References to the Pacific Ocean appear in rooflines that carry the shape of gentle breaking waves, a rhythmic procession that brings order to the design. A dramatic column-free terminal suffused with natural daylight acknowledges the area's temperate climate, while views recognize the presence of both the ocean to the west and the Santa Monica Mountains to the east.

While accentuating the future of the city, the Fentress design also respects the architecture of the past, sparked by the once-futuristic 1961 Theme Building designed by William Pereira.

"Pereira has always been one of my favorite architects," says Fentress. "The Theme Building is a historic landmark. There was no mandate as to how to relate to it, but I think our forms for the waves are sympathetic to the Theme Building's curves. Arches support the two-level bridges connecting the terminal, pick up that architectural vocabulary, and amplify it through the vision of the master plan."

The Theme Building, which has undergone a major restoration, now is loved for its retro charm and Modernist lines; the same cannot be said for the rest of LAX.

Over the years, plans to modernize the airport – which is locked in its current boundaries – were discussed, but fell victim to political pressures. At the time the modernization commission was announced, the airport's star had grown dim, according to polls of the traveling public. The design magazine *Dwell* voted LAX the world's worst airport, describing it as "a collection of drab terminals linked by a traffic jam." All that Jet Age cachet of the Theme Building seemed to be left behind.

Loss of status was not just a matter of bruised civic pride. Economics were key: each international flight into LA generates more than $620 million a year in income, so losing these millions to other coastal cities was not an option.

Area residents, when asked to describe Los Angeles, repeatedly mentioned the natural beauty, the ocean and the beaches, which inspired the flowing curves of the Bradley West modernization. The once-futuristic Theme Building (right) also lends design elements to the plan.

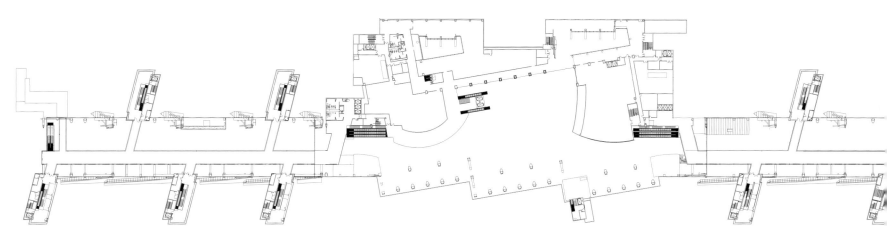

FLOOR PLAN

Along with improved amenities, the modernization is intended to address other challenges. International passengers will find a welcoming environment. Fifteen new gates are designed to accommodate the new breed of super-sized jets, the A380 and the Dreamliner 787. Circulation will make sense. The time-consuming process of busing passengers to the Bradley Terminal and marching them through a dark, windowless corridor to immigration will be a thing of the past.

But at heart, the project pivots on the satisfaction of each person who uses the place.

"Our design is all about the passenger experience. We think about that over and over as we design. This is where we come into our own as architects. We want clear and easy-to-understand circulation, where you can see where you are going intuitively. A gracious, open space, a building filled with daylight. It is a matter of sustainability, but also good physiologically. For people drawn by the sun and the beach, it brings LA inside."

All that's missing is the sand.

*

In 2009, Los Angeles International Airport served 56 million passengers, against a capacity of 40 million. There are 153 gates.

(Left and following spread) A pedestrian bridge, concourses and other elements of LAX echo the shape of waves.

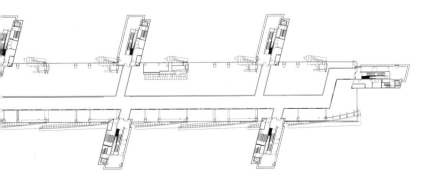

BACK TO THE FUTURE

Los Angeles is known for many things, most of them related to glitter and celebrity. Mid-century Modern architecture also is a powerful draw to this city, and that begins right at the gateway known as LAX. The elevated Theme Building is a mix of Modern and retro, futuristic and sleek, and a symbol of innovation and postwar optimism. Then the 1961 Theme Building fell on hard times, when a chunk fell off and landed on a structure nearby. It became the subject of a $12.3-million renovation and seismic retrofitting in which a tuned mass damper was installed at the top to promote stability. Completed in early 2010 by the architecture firm of Gin Wong Associates, the project has put this lyrical, arched icon on track for another half century. Just like the airport around it.

Project **Terminals A, B, C, Consolidated Rental Car Facility, Roadways**
Location **San Jose, California**
Owner **Norman Y. Mineta San Jose International Airport**
Year **2010**

Curtis Fentress "The computer has changed forever how people connect. San Jose is in the heart of Silicon Valley. So for the airport in San Jose, we worked with the concept of a co-axial computer cable. What better way to match the challenges presented by a long, linear site?"

4

SJC

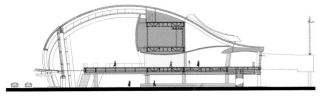

SECTION

San Jose International Airport Terminal B's new curved roof design incorporates patterned glass to mediate the light.

From the desktops and laptops we write on, to phones that do much more than dial a number, computers have transformed the way we work and play. The brains behind this revolution, the concentration of research labs, high-tech incubators, and lone-wolf inventors in California's Santa Clara Valley, have given this one-time agricultural haven a new name: Silicon Valley. And if this topography of the mind can have a capital, it is San Jose.

Located south of the Bay Area, San Jose's airport jousts with fields in San Francisco and Oakland for its share of the travel market. But even as the airline business has faced challenges from booming fuel prices and busted travel counts, officials of the Norman Y. Mineta San Jose International Airport realized that modernization was key for the future.

That presented Fentress with a complicated design project, where demolition and construction had to occur while the airport continued to operate at full strength. Smart phasing, teamwork, and the introduction of shared-use gates and ticket counters smoothed the way toward creating a new look and more intuitive circulation for San Jose.

Fentress' design principles rely heavily on the concepts of culture and context, creating public buildings that connect to place, people and history, and that cultivate unity and respect.

"Each of our airports speaks to the place, the culture, and the people there," Fentress says. "It's the way a community thinks, the way they relate to the rest of the world."

In considering a design for the San Jose airport, Fentress faced the same kind of cultural dichotomy found at Raleigh-Durham International Airport. On one hand, San Jose, like the Research Triangle area of North Carolina, thrives on its reputation for research and innovation. Yet just as that region of North Carolina is rich in the work of artisans and craftspeople, San Jose shares an agricultural past with much of California. In a different life, the city was known for its orchards and vineyards.

At the same time, the San Jose design-build project also relied on split-second coordination: Terminal A received a major renovation, while Terminal C underwent an interim modification until it could be razed to clear space for Terminal B. Also part of the project is the construction of a consolidated rental car garage, which includes public parking and improvements to roads and parking areas. All of this took place on a narrow, linear site constrained by existing waterways, highways and runways – around an operational airport.

The centerpiece of this logistical challenge is Terminal B, where Fentress expressed the disparate ideas of high-tech industry and nature's bounty in subtle yet surprising ways. The sinuous exterior takes the form of an articulated tube, with generous glass curtain walls broken by stretches of ribbed or perforated metal skin. Like a coaxial cable rolled out for use, the building reflects a sense of layering, a rhythm achieved by texture.

The tube-within-a-tube form of Terminal B sports a skin that picks up rhythm from sections of glass and metal. This articulation allows the walls to flex sideways, offering increased seismic protection.

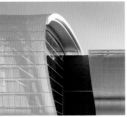

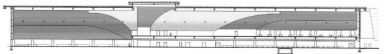

WALL ELEVATION

While the media called this airport the most innovative in the U.S., San Jose's design relies on the simplicity of the "kiss-and-fly" concept, where travelers can be dropped off, head through security, and quickly reach their gates.

Through the use of different types of glass, with the metal mesh, Fentress achieves dramatic effects in the quality of light to remind travelers of the natural setting. First is the wash of daylight into the large public spaces, a hallmark of the studio's design ethos. But the effects produced by the interplay of light and structure, what the Japanese call *komorebi*, recall the dappled light found on a walk through orchards or forests, where trees filter sunlight into intriguing forms. This impression is created by sections of the terminal's outer walls and by filtering light through skylights. That is especially true in the area leading from the North Concourse into Terminal B, where patterned glass casts unexpected shadows on people walking below.

As befits a region that thrives on the buzz of new technology and innovation, the new terminal includes numerous high-tech features that improve travel for both passengers and airlines.

Instead of standard-issue seats, travelers now relax in inventive chairs that both offer comfort and allow people to work while waiting. Zenky Air Chairs by Zoeftig include an integrated air cooling and

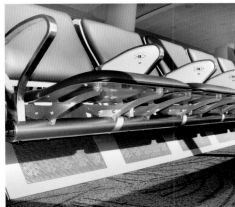

A light-filled Terminal enhances passenger comfort and convenience (left and top), including the installation of innovative Zenky Air Chairs by Zoeftig. The seating includes an integrated air cooling and heating system, positioned unobtrusively in the chair's base.

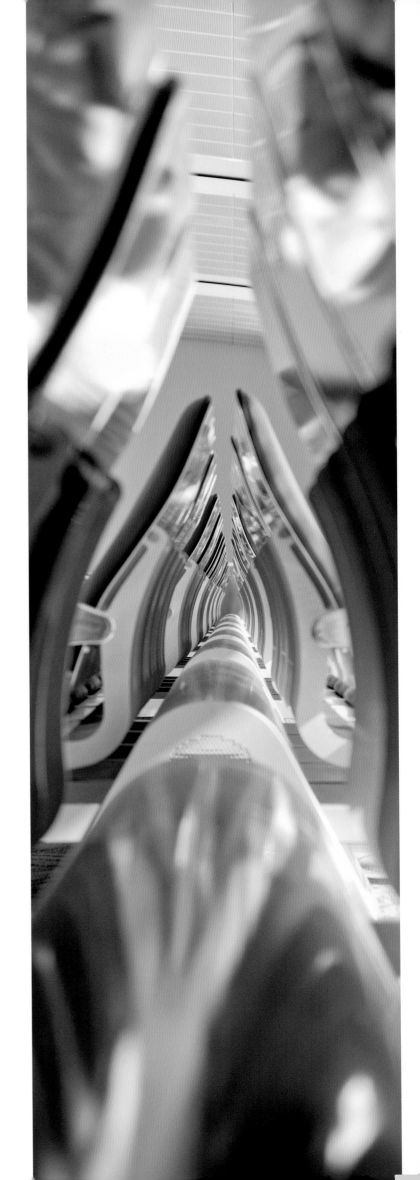

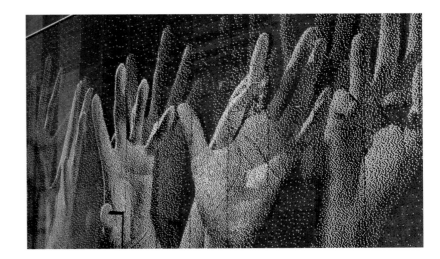

heating system, positioned unobtrusively in the chair's base, and come equipped with built-in power and USB ports. A digital paging system features flat-screen panels that show text messages. A dozen screening machines capable of body scans are part of the new security system, as are new state-of-the-art baggage scanners – the most advanced technology in the world. More than three acres of solar panels top the consolidated rental car facility, or ConRAC, providing enough power for that building and for hundreds of homes.

Even some of the public art is rooted in high-tech aesthetics: Bjoern Schuelke's sculptural installation *Space Observer* records and displays videos, diverting travelers who pass by its futuristic "body." In contrast, artist Christian Moeller's *Hands*, which wraps the rental car facility, is based on the old-fashioned definition of "digital." The hands are those of numerous San Jose residents.

The terminal project is grounded in technology that meets advanced seismic standards, a crucial element of any building in California and one that here is built into the refined design.

"We designed an innovative roof that can slide 14 inches in either direction to withstand seismic activity, at the same time creating a sleek, artistic profile," says Fentress.

*

Norman Y. Mineta San Jose International Airport, completed in 2010, has a capacity of 14 million passengers and operates 28 fixed gates.

The new consolidated rental car facility, or ConRAC, is adjacent to the new Terminal B, embraced by the largest public art piece to date in San Jose. Artist Christian Moeller's textural *Hands* is created from 3-inch caps embedded in a mesh fence that wraps the building.

SEATTLE-TACOMA INTERNATIONAL AIRPORT

Project **Central Terminal Expansion and Redevelopment**
Location **Seattle, Washington**
Owner **Port of Seattle**
Year **2005**

Curtis Fentress "The airport needed a new heart. We designed a 'town center' to connect the concourses, to create a natural flow, with a vital pulse."

5
SEA

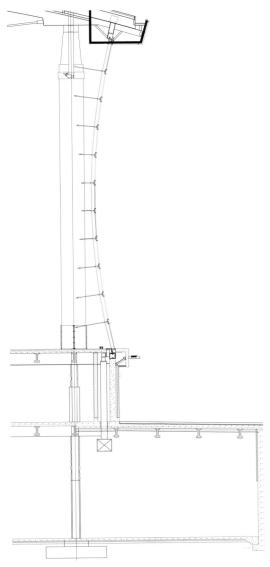

CURTAIN WALL DETAIL

At Seattle-Tacoma International Airport, the Central Terminal's innovative curtain wall is wrap-around glass, curved in two directions to afford panoramic views.

The people of Seattle and Tacoma have crafted a culture that speaks to the beauty of the Northwest, a style of living where the physical environment is cherished as much as the usual attractions of urban life.

For years, the region's airport was a working facility designed for much more simple times. But that was before air travel became a more vulnerable pursuit, a growing cautionary tale that culminated in the attacks of 9/11. This made navigation between concourses impossible without going through security. It became a cumbersome trek, and left Seattle-Tacoma International Airport a place with no real core, no centerpiece to serve travelers.

The airport also did not reflect the vitality of the cities it served, where cultural amenities, locally grown foods, intriguing places to shop, and nature help define a region. When Fentress won the commission to expand and redevelop the central terminal, it became apparent that while improving circulation was key, so was bringing a sense of place to the airport.

"The Pacific Marketplace became the airport's heart," says Curtis Fentress. "We looked at the outdoor marketplaces throughout Seattle and Tacoma that had become centers of the community. That's what was needed here."

Fentress landed the Sea-Tac commission after designing Denver International Airport and Incheon International Airport, both greenfield airports built on undeveloped sites. The Sea-Tac Central Terminal was another matter entirely, and became the first in

Seen from airside (top), the glass wall brings inside the rhythm and romance of aircraft taking off and landing, recalling observation decks of the past. The structure also pulls together existing sections of the airport (site plan, right).

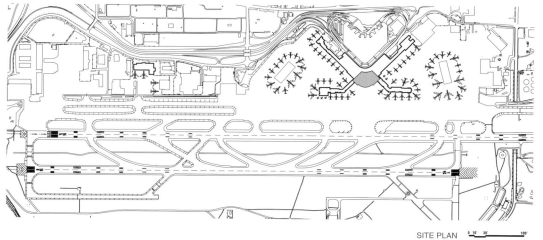

SITE PLAN   0 10' 30'   100'

a series of Fentress airport projects that involved expansion and redevelopment basically on top of an existing and operating facility. Although that means building a new structure while the airport is fully functioning, in the case of Sea-Tac, perhaps the most challenging piece of the puzzle was introducing heightened passenger amenities. Better dining and shopping were a priority, as was the introduction of public engagement – more to do and see – and improved practical aspects of air travel. In addition, the redevelopment used the new building to create a seismic brace for the 1950s control tower.

"The coolest thing about Sea-Tac is the glass curtain wall, and the development of the double-curved cable net, so that it is curved in plan and in section," says principal Ned Kirschbaum. "At first, we designed the glass wall this way to reduce deflections. But we ended up minimizing the structure to maximize the views and bring the outdoors in. It has the sense of an outdoor marketplace. It's an elegant design. That, to us, is so important."

This open-air impression defines the Great Hall of the Pacific Marketplace, which was inspired by the famed Pike Place Market and numerous farmer's markets in both cities. This 130,000-square-foot multi-purpose hall is a pioneering example of airport branding.

The Marketplace's skin is a soaring curtain wall made of bi-directional curved glass; that is, a length of glass that manages to arc in two directions at the same time. The 60-foot-tall vertical span is convex, while the 350-foot-long horizontal stretch is concave. This giant glass shield runs parallel to the airport's runways, offering visitors a view of not just the normal airport buzz – planes landing and taking off every minute – but also a lens on the region's natural features and weather activity.

It is a place intended for grabbing a meal, finding a chair, reading a book, opening a laptop, and watching people go by — a public space that is about connecting with each other or stealing a chance to take a deep breath. Passengers know that a large arrivals and departures display sign is right there for keeping tabs on flights, and that the appropriate concourse is nearby. It was time to put a "there" there, and the new Pacific Marketplace went beyond mere physical setting. It's where the public measures the airport's vital signs.

*

In 2009, Seattle-Tacoma International Airport served 31.2 million passengers, with a capacity of 45 million. There are 93 gates.

The Pacific Marketplace is part dining room, part living room, and all natural light. Ralph Helmick and Stuart Schechter's suspended mixed-media sculpture *Landing* presides over the activity and depicts an abstracted image of a bird reflected in a pond.

RALEIGH-DURHAM INTERNATIONAL AIRPORT

Project **Terminal 2 and Concourse Redevelopment**
Location **Raleigh-Durham, North Carolina**
Client **Raleigh-Durham Airport Authority**
Year **Phase I: 2008 Phase 2: 2011**

Curtis Fentress "The theme, the real essence of RDU, is hand-made, mind-made. You have the brain power at the universities – North Carolina, North Carolina State and Duke, the Research Triangle, and the research facilities they have created. And you still have the history of the place, the crafts of the region, and the rolling hills."

RDU

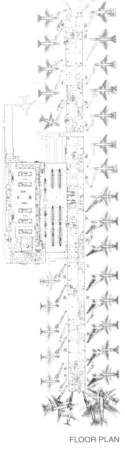

FLOOR PLAN

Northorth Carolina is the kind of place that stays with you, no matter where you might live. The beauty of the land, from the mountains to the Atlantic Ocean, the fine craftsmanship, the famed Southern hospitality – it's all ingrained in those who've called North Carolina home.

Curtis Fentress' vision for the Terminal 2 replacement at Raleigh-Durham International Airport bears witness to that. Fentress was born, raised, and educated in North Carolina, and stayed close to his roots even after graduating from the College of Design at North Carolina State University and starting a career in New York. The culture and place are part of him, so it was natural that his design for a new terminal for RDU would reflect the region's soul.

Which explains the paradox at work at RDU.

On one hand, this is a place where crafts and a legacy of making things – from fabric to musical instruments to furniture – are creative and economic forces. Yet this airport – situated between Duke University, North Carolina State University, and the University of North Carolina – is also home to some of the most high-tech and innovative industries and research facilities in the world, spurred by the founding in the 1950s of Research Triangle Park. Indigenous crafts and forward-thinking design may appear to hail from different universes, but this reflects the duality of today's society: high-tech meets high-touch, or "hand-made and mind-made."

When Fentress won the commission to design RDU, the phased project posed the operational challenge of serving almost nine million people a year who must use this important regional gateway during construction, day in and day out.

Fentress' knowledge of the two sides of the cultural reality allowed him to balance the innately mechanical nature of a giant public facility with elements that reference the impact of natural resources and the human hand. An innovative example of this is the unusual use of wood in the terminal, in the form of lenticular trusses made of laminated Douglas fir. While the trusses shape and support the curvilinear roof in a way that creates column-free spaces, covering spans up to 160 feet long, the material also recalls the state's wooded countryside.

"The theme of the rolling hills is expressed in the roof. Using wood beams brought the crafts and the hardwoods into the building, giving it a warmth and a feeling of Carolinian and Southern hospitality," Fentress says. "No other major airport in America has wood beams in the ceilings. This airport is warm and inviting and distinctly of its place."

The choice of the laminated lenticular trusses for the roof structure added a level of complexity for the design team. "This was true from a structural, fire protection and detailing perspective," says principal Tom Theobald. "The Fentress team worked closely with our structural engineers to design each connection detail to reinforce our concept of a 'crafted' building. We worked closely with North Carolina State University's materials testing lab to study the strength of the wood-to-steel connections. We built full-scale mock-ups and took them to failure, which gave everyone greater confidence that the system would perform. This attention to detail has resulted in an efficient and beautiful roof truss design."

The studio's ingrained philosophy of passenger convenience is evident in the new terminal. Airline counters are located in the middle of the lobby in an island design, a move to ease congestion. The design also looks to the future, pioneering the implementation of common-use systems, which allow airlines to share ticket counters, check-in kiosks, gates and other airport operations.

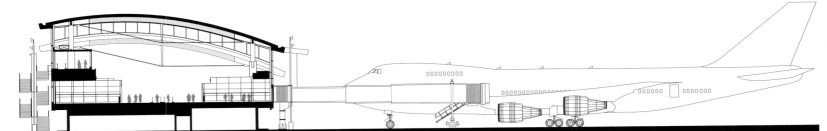

CONCOURSE SECTION

The generous use of glass in clerestories brings
abundant light to boarding areas. The rolling hills of
North Carolina inspired the gently curved roofs.

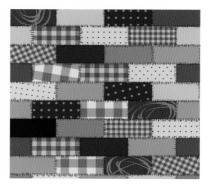

Laminated Douglas fir trusses envelop the RDU terminal (facing page), keying off North Carolina's strong tradition of crafts, musical instruments, and furniture production. Metal truss connectors (left) bring stability and a high-tech edge to the wood's warm sensibility.

A cross-section shows details of the airport from airside to curbside (right).

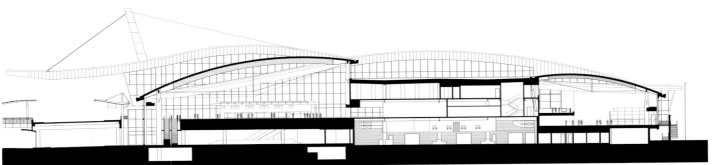

TICKET HALL BUILDING SECTION

In the end, saving time and money through flexibility is crucial to making the experience of traveling more of a pleasure and less of a grind. That may be a new definition of North Carolina hospitality.

*

Raleigh-Durham International Airport in 2009 served 8.9 million passengers, against a capacity of 11.4 million. The completion of Phase I resulted in 19 additional gates; Phase II will add 13 more for a total of 32 gates.

Material innovation and exploration of form are crucial elements in avant-garde fashion design. This is often dramatic, technologically and culturally advanced couture, provocative – controversial even. As in architectural design, each work is carefully handled from concept to execution, drawing from the principles of artistic inspiration as well as technical precision.

Every design, whether architectural or fashion, carries myriad aesthetic and cultural references. Through fabric, form, shape, and movement, the essence is portrayed in one final product to be inhabited, or worn, by the human body. Curtis Fentress' design for the Incheon International Airport in Seoul, South Korea, draws from cultural cues and contextual references that ultimately inform the massive space with a sense of local artistry infused with warmth and comfort.

This takes into consideration the human experience. Curved walls bring in light as a functional element, but also to echo nature. A project is completed, but beyond this, a sense of place is created. Innovative design changes the way we perceive our experience, forcing us to take notice and pay attention. It offers the possibility to enhance, or enable, our way of life.

Buildings and clothing provide shelter, comfort and support. Beyond these basic functions, there is an endless amount of freedom on the part of the designer to create his or her own vision of the world. Airports and clothing are fundamentally pragmatic in nature. They become more than just an object or a place through a dedication to innovation and design.

Fentress' design for the passenger terminal complex at Denver International Airport began with the simple concept of encompassing light. The innovative use of fabric on the roof created a sense of harmony with the natural surroundings. The expressive, emotive design welcomes visitors to dream, explore and reflect. It affects the way viewers experience the space, and how they move through it.

Instilling a deep sense of imagination into design requires a dedication to technology and innovation – constantly pushing the boundaries in order to explore new ideas. At DIA's Terminal, Fentress employed expansive glass walls that let in the prevalent Colorado light and offered views of the outdoors, while enhancing the project's sustainability, passenger comfort and experience.

A willingness to explore materials and form is echoed in the work of British designer Alexander McQueen. Though his career was cut short by his shocking suicide, he spent nearly two decades creating some of the most stimulating designs in the fashion world. His beginnings with the famed Saville Row tailors of London gave him not just the fundamental understanding of the gestures necessary to work with fabric; this training also set free untamable creativity. This incredibly talented fashion designer broke all the design codes, if there were any. Like Fentress, McQueen focused on detail. This acute attention and precision followed him throughout his career.

While McQueen was a young master's student at Central St. Martin's, his entire collection was purchased by the late, illustrious *Vogue* editor Isabella Blow. This began a lasting friendship between the two, and launched McQueen as a star. He quickly became something of an *enfant terrible*, and grew to be associated with an aesthetic full of drama, rebellion and futuristic tendencies. His fashion shows were theatrical and lively. McQueen's clothing constantly reflects the same sense of technological innovation as Fentress, employing new fabrics, skills and shapes in diverse ways.

McQueen's prodigious output and drive for perfection recalls the work of Curtis Fentress, who as a young man realized his enthusiasm for the field of architecture and has continued to demonstrate his commitment to innovative, sustainable and timeless design. Both are recognized for works that explore deep, passionate, dramatic, and theatrical elements. The two artists were lauded, respectively, for their unique and bold sense of composition — McQueen's fundamental understanding of the body, and Fentress' command of public spaces.

Though some McQueen designs reveled in their outrageous constructions or accessories, his clothing actually is comfortable. If some designers' couture pieces are like wearing a piece of armor, McQueen's structural savvy, talent at cutting (done without a pattern, but by instinct), and ability to construct a garment resulted in a piece that was as easy to wear as it is beautiful. It was his secret, honed during years of the kind of practice that can result in star power.

McQueen's mastery of shape and form comes across in his ability to adapt. Fentress' design for Denver International Airport is meant to "work with structure, work with form, and work with the building to express something that is not too literal." Such a conceptual approach to design is deeply echoed by fashion designers such as McQueen.

As our culture becomes increasingly reliant upon technology, these innovations allow the architecture and fashion design communities to explore in a profound manner the realm of material, movement and space.

COLORADO CONVENTION CENTER
PASADENA CONVENTION CENTER
PALM SPRINGS CONVENTION CENTER
SANTA FE COMMUNITY CONVENTION CENTER

2

CONVENTI
CENTERS

CONVENTION
CENTERS

Who hasn't spent hours in a windowless, seemingly lifeless meeting room, with no connection to the rest of the city? That's the way it feels to spend a day in most American convention centers, those big bland boxes plopped into place in so many cities. Throughout the country, convention centers and airports rank as the strongest economic drivers of their respective cities, crucial elements in how areas brand themselves and their cultural and retail attractions.

Yet convention centers often turn their backs on life outside, forgetting that an active urban environment is a major determinant in how conference organizers choose the location for an event.

Fentress convention center designs are distinguished by their transparency, linking the urban activity outside with the meetings and exhibitions inside. In this section, you will tour some of the studio's designs, where abundant light and the sensitive use of glass offers comfort to people who otherwise might feel as if they were cut off from what is going on outside.

Meanwhile, Fentress seeks ways to weave large public halls into day-to-day life downtown. Not only does this strengthen a city's urban design, it also connects visitors to amenities throughout the city, making their stay more fun while generating revenue for area merchants. A basic premise of a Fentress convention center is to incorporate the meeting facility into the activity around it, and the community as a whole.

Fentress' expertise in convention center design is not limited to building from the ground up. The studio also understands how to transform old, outmoded centers into vibrant and flexible gathering places, designed to deliver one unified architectural statement. By definition, convention centers are large buildings – the Colorado Convention Center fills nine city blocks – but Fentress designs interior spaces to achieve a human scale. After all, these are places designed for people.

COLORADO CONVENTION CENTER

Location **Denver, Colorado**
Owner **City and County of Denver**
Year **2004**

Curtis Fentress "This is a true urban public building. It is a convention center that connects with the city's major performing art spaces and all of downtown. So it becomes one big venue for tourism and entertainment and the public."

1

When Fentress' expanded Colorado Convention Center opened in 2004, the era of the proverbial "box with a dock" had come to an end. Instead, this was a place that redefined the city's skyline, with bold silver blades and mega-curtain walls that shined a light on Denver. It didn't shut the city out; it called the city over for a visit.

Even when the original Colorado Convention Center opened in 1990, also designed by Fentress, plans were in place to double the size of the building. As the years passed, and the city saw bigger venues snag bigger conferences, it became clear Denver needed a larger convention center. Perhaps more importantly, trends had changed regarding convention center design and amenities: Instead of regarding windows as a source of distraction for those attending a convention, meeting planners understood that tapping into the healthful qualities of natural light could enliven meetings and those stuck in them all day.

First, though, step back a bit: in November 1999, Denver residents showed uncommon generosity, voting to approve almost $400 million in bonds to expand the convention center, fund improvements to the Denver Zoo, and build a new wing for the Denver Art Museum.

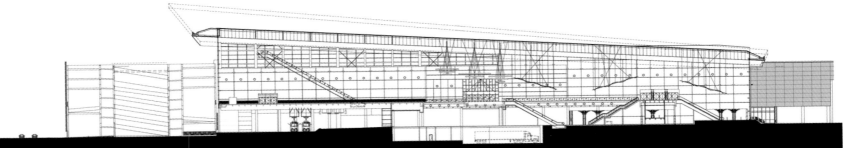

SECTION

The expanded Colorado Convention Center helps unify Denver's downtown core through its reach to Speer Boulevard, a busy diagonal thoroughfare and a major connector through the city. The Speer façade blade points the way to the Denver Performing Arts Complex and the mountains.

The Colorado Convention Center is a key downtown transit-oriented development, since light rail runs through it, linking a station at the convention center and downtown to the metro area. The site plan (facing page) indicates entry points and connections within a facility that covers nine city blocks.

Abundant city-sponsored public art is incorporated into the building, including Lawrence Argent's popular *I See What You Mean*, better known as the Big Blue Bear (facing page).

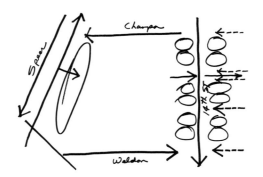

Choices made that day extended a decade of dramatic physical expansion that delivered Denver into a new millennium. But the impact of the expanded Colorado Convention Center went beyond bringing bigger meetings and more people to fill hotel rooms and buy meals. The center, which covers nine city blocks, increased its role as a catalyst for development along a once-barren 14th Street in the Central Business District. The convention center also helped pull together downtown: it connects the important Speer Boulevard corridor to urban core activity, creates a link with the city's performing arts center, and is an example of a transit-oriented development with major reach, since it shelters a light-rail station in the heart of the city. Finally, the convention center dramatically changed the city's skyline, with the excitement inherent in a picture postcard view.

The program for the expanded convention center called for doubling the amount of space for exhibitions to 600,000 square feet, and adding more space for registration in order to accommodate several conventions at the same time. Selected by the city in a design competition, Fentress faced the challenge of adding a 5,000-seat auditorium and a 1,000-space parking garage to the mix. The original

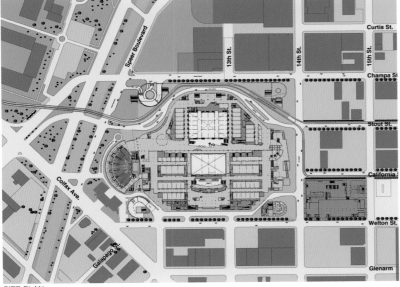

SITE PLAN

center had only one active "front door." The expansion needed two working entries, and the ability to better connect the new convention hall to the 16th Street Mall, the city's vital commercial, pedestrian and transportation spine.

"In the design of the building, we intentionally created two very strong glassy façades," says Curtis Fentress. "The one on 14th Street was welcoming for conventioneers to come into the building and was very transparent, open and accessible. You could see where you were going, and you knew where the conventions were. On the Speer Boulevard side, we took advantage of the fact that people would be coming out of the ballroom and wanted to give them a dramatic view of the mountains."

Fentress skillfully tucked the old convention center into a new wrapping of stainless steel skin and panoramic glass curtain walls, including one that stretches 800 feet long – the length of an 80-story building lying on its side. Dramatic cantilevered metal blades reach out toward Speer Boulevard and 14th Street, welcoming visitors and allowing uplighting to make the building glow on the skyline, while shielding the interior from harsh afternoon sun.

Rather than close one street, Fentress turned it into a curvy chicane, in the process allowing the light-rail station to slide under the convention center.

"The convention center is a truly integrated transportation-oriented development," Fentress says. "That gave the city a covered station in the middle of the convention center, and connects to hotels and to residents in the suburbs. This made it a better convention venue."

And one able to weave together a city's many parts.

The Wells Fargo Theater (above) hosts public concerts and lectures, as well as events held in conjunction with conventions. The auditorium's flexibility rests on being divisible, as well as having its own lobby and entry (above right). The elevation along Welton Street runs from 14th Street to the auditorium on Speer Boulevard (right).

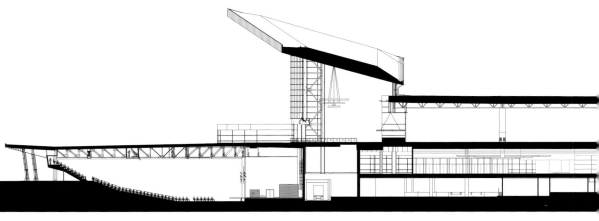

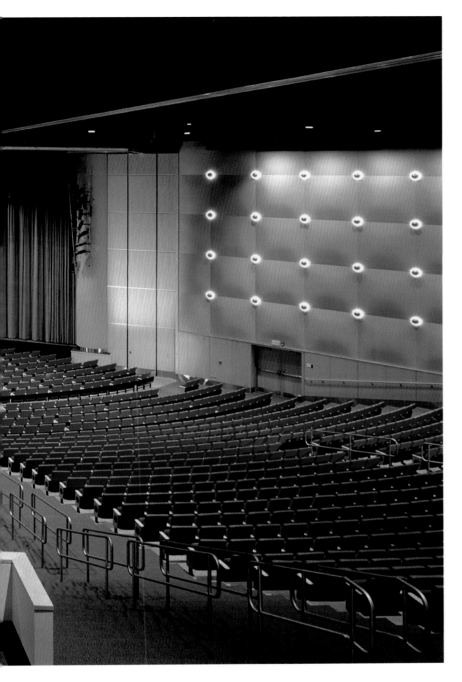

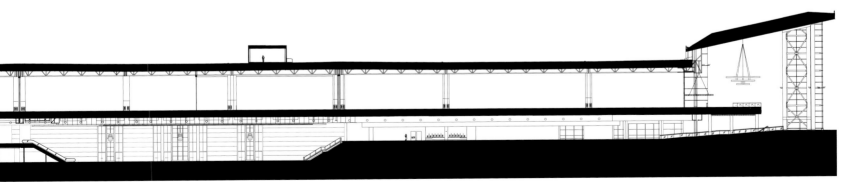

SECTION

A parking garage integrated into the Colorado Convention Center (left) also serves visitors to the nearby performing arts complex. Like the rest of the convention center's skin, the garage and ramp are accented by undulating strips of perforated metal, which both enliven the complex and diminish its bulk. Terraces and balconies give visitors an opportunity to savor Colorado's good weather.

MAJOR ECONOMIC BOOSTER

Most downtown civic projects are touted as major development boosts to the neighborhood, often an area that has seen better times and brighter revenues. The Colorado Convention Center hit a home run, since the 2004 expansion created a powerful ripple effect on improvements in Denver's downtown core.

Soon after the new center opened, its impact became clear: the city gained four hotels and two residential towers. An old municipal auditorium was transformed into a glittering opera house, becoming one of nine venues under the umbrella of the Denver Performing Arts Complex, where 10,000 seats await lovers of theater, music and dance. The convention center expansion dug deep into the city's commercial heart, bringing new economic vitality. How vital? Convention center activity alone has pumped over $2.2 billion into the city's economy since the building opened. Its neighbors have responded: in 2009, owners along 14th from Lower Downtown to the Civic Center area agreed to contribute $4 million to enhance the streetscape and maintenance.

Panoramic glass curtain walls and gleaming, uplighted blades give the Colorado Convention Center a presence on the Denver skyline – day and night. This visibility helps visitors easily find entries to the convention center and the light-rail station.

PASADENA CONVENTION CENTER

Location **Pasadena, California**
Client **Pasadena Center Operating Company**
Year **2009**

Curtis Fentress "We wanted the two new convention center buildings to be bookends to the Pasadena Civic Auditorium, to pick up the rhythm and carry it into the architecture. It's as if you had the theme of a piece of music in the middle, and on each side, architecturally, you had the beginning and the end of the music. But you let this piece in the middle be the crescendo."

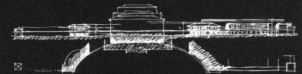

Art, music, theater and entertainment are deeply rooted in Pasadena, home to the Rose Bowl Parade and, for years, the Emmy Awards and People's Choice Awards. At the heart of this confluence of culture and glitz is the Pasadena Civic Auditorium, a community treasure and a landmark in Pasadena's urban core.

For years, this 1932 Mediterranean Revival building, with elegant Beaux Arts elements, looked like Cinderella flanked by two ugly stepsisters. The buildings were parts of a 1975 convention center mainly set underground, perceived by visitors as two pillbox-style structures whose entrances were difficult to decipher.

Replacing and expanding these unsympathetic structures was a task that called for more than just expertise in designing a large and complex public building. It also required the sensitivity to design a new convention center that enhanced the civic auditorium while linking it more closely to the rest of the city.

The Pasadena Center Operating Company selected Fentress for the job, knowing the studio was adept at balancing old and new, and creating strong and welcoming entries. Sustainability in construction techniques, materials and operation led to a center that has achieved LEED Gold certification from the U.S. Green Building Council.

PASADENA CONVENTION CENTER HIGHLIGHTED

The Pasadena Civic Auditorium (left) has played host to some of the most glittering events in America. The new Pasadena Convention Center now flanks the historic building, which was an anchor of noted planner Edward H. Bennett's 1920s plan for a civic center in Pasadena. Aerial view (left) shows the relationship of old and new buildings and their entries.

Overlaying and extending horizontal and vertical elements of the civic auditorium determined scale and massing for the new convention center. The datum lines served as a "score" for the design (following spread).

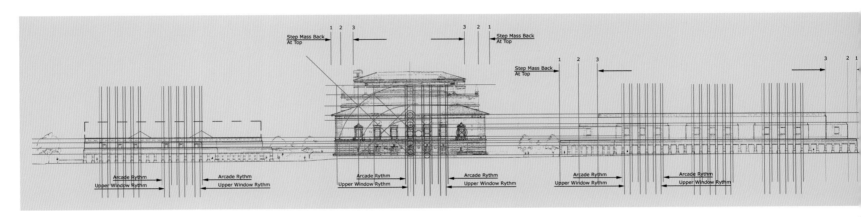

For a solution, Fentress turned to a major activity at the civic auditorium: music. In drawings made during the conceptual period of design, horizontal datum lines define the various components of the building, providing a guide toward establishing the proportions and articulation of the new convention center's architectural personality. It's as if a musical score were placed over the three structures, lining up important reference points and setting up a rhythm that allows the buildings to work in harmony.

"We felt the Pasadena Convention Center needed to respond to the urban context," says Fentress. "We wanted to create a street front much more open and accessible to the people of Pasadena and that adhered more to the original 1920s Civic Center plan by Edward H. Bennett."

Fentress' reliance on restraint as a design principle helped guide the vision of a new convention center that embraces the signature building. The new buildings offer easily understandable entryways, complement the civic auditorium in color palette and architectural vocabulary, and connect to the city's other amenities. The convention center also respects the city's foundation: the master plan by noted Chicago-based planner Bennett places the auditorium as the anchor on the southern edge of the civic plaza.

The layout offers the flexibility needed to handle events of all sizes, another characteristic of a Fentress convention center. The studio placed a 55,000-square-foot exhibition hall on one side of the auditorium, a space that can be divided into two rooms or used in conjunction with the 25,000-square-foot ballroom, for larger events. The convention center, on the other side of the auditorium, includes 28,000 square feet of meeting rooms and 25,000 square feet of space for registration and pre-function activities.

These two sections of the convention center appear to curve out to the street, reaching out to visitors while creating a generous plaza. For the convention center, this space takes advantage of Pasadena's temperate climate to form a link between inside and outside for gatherings. For the civic auditorium, with its rich lineup of glittering red-carpet events, access to a 22,000-square-foot outdoor "room" is like throwing its doors open to the city, so history and the arts can come together to play.

An entry lobby at the Pasadena Convention Center, marked by custom-designed chandeliers, opens up to a spacious plaza to allow functions both indoors and outdoors, benefiting from Pasadena's temperate climate.

A section drawing of the convention center building devoted to exhibition space and a ballroom shows the flexibility and ease of circulation for those attending conferences and banquets (right). The convention center's stone façade gives off a golden glow at night, lighting up this popular part of Pasadena (following spread).

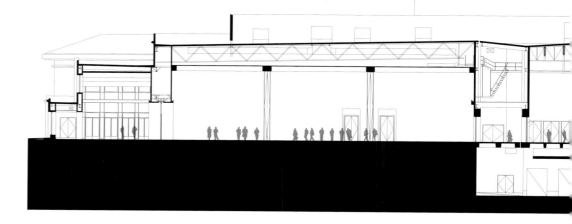

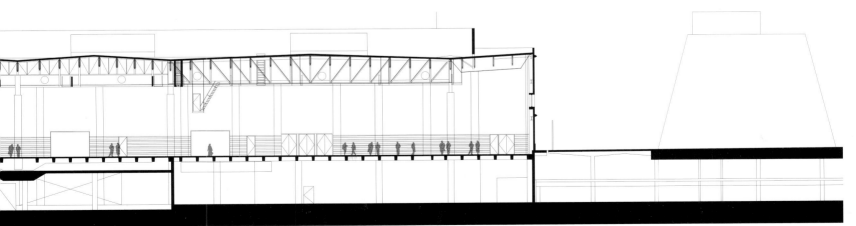

SECTION

DESIGNING A CITY

Architect and planner Edward H. Bennett may be best known as co-author of Daniel Burnham's 1909 groundbreaking *Plan of Chicago.* Just as Chicago is known for its influence on architecture nationwide, the city also exported early expertise in the field of urban design.

Bennett devised comprehensive plans for cities such as Portland and Minneapolis, and civic centers in Denver, where his concepts were put in place in 1917, and later, in Pasadena. His 1923 plan for Pasadena stressed the importance of the axis, organizing civic buildings such as a Central Library, City Hall and Civic Auditorium in a pleasing ensemble. The auditorium now serves as centerpiece for the new Pasadena Convention Center.

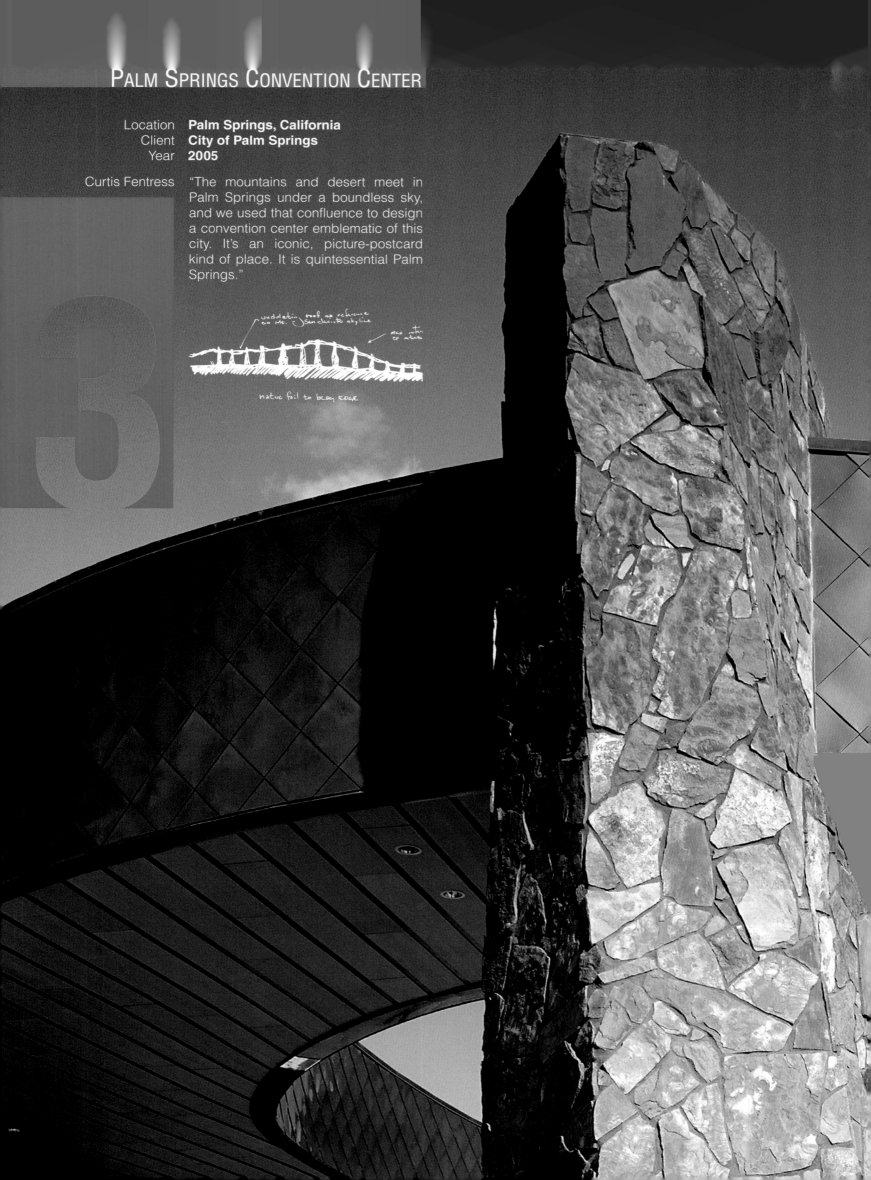

PALM SPRINGS CONVENTION CENTER

Location **Palm Springs, California**
Client **City of Palm Springs**
Year **2005**

Curtis Fentress "The mountains and desert meet in Palm Springs under a boundless sky, and we used that confluence to design a convention center emblematic of this city. It's an iconic, picture-postcard kind of place. It is quintessential Palm Springs."

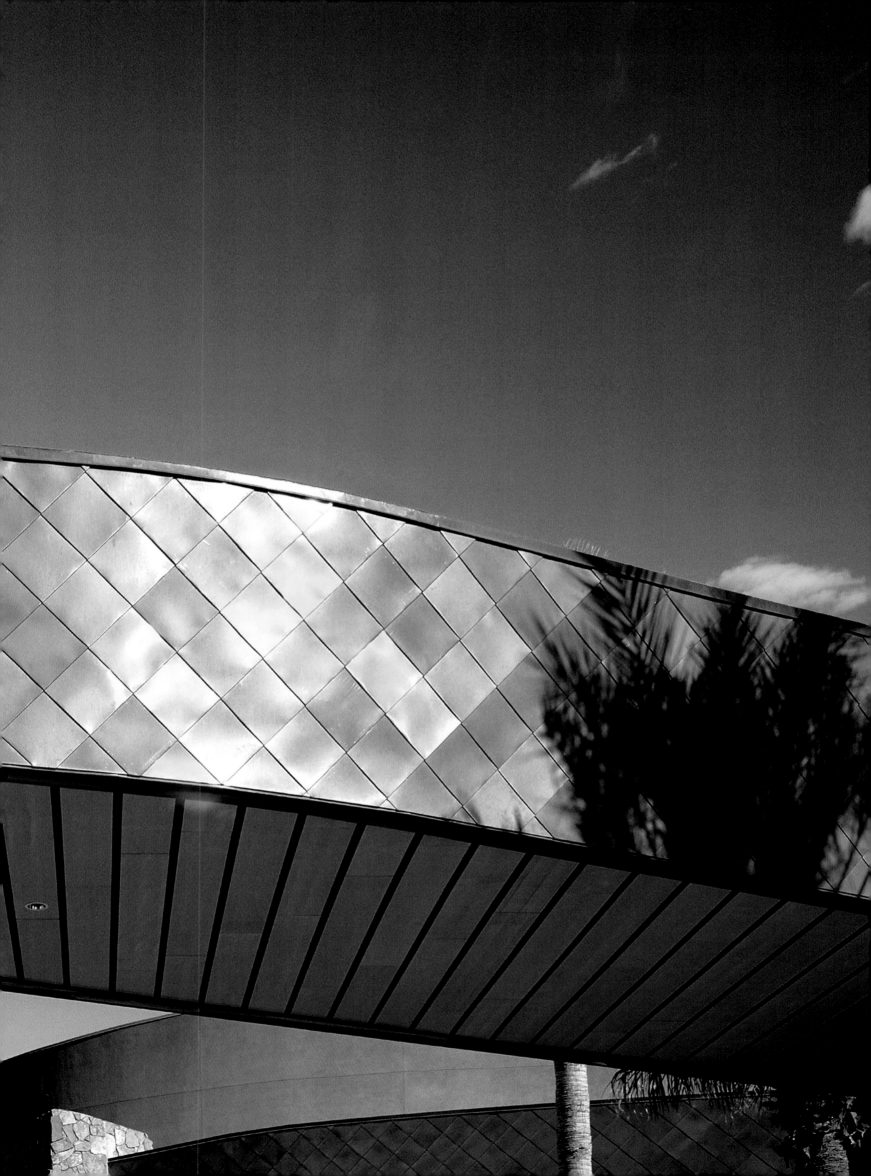

The natural beauty of Palm Springs informs everything about this Southern California city, a place that for decades has attracted those seeking solace and good health, in a setting equally made for play.

That includes those attending conventions here, who encountered a 1985 building that sported an indifferent appearance and a front door that turned its back on the city.

When officials in Palm Springs selected Fentress to design a new convention center, "We moved the front door to reorient the building, create a closer relationship with Palm Springs, and frame views of the mountains," says Mike Winters, principal.

The original entrance had been on the side of the building away from Palm Canyon Drive, the heart of the city's restaurants, hotels and casinos. By flipping the plan of the convention center, Fentress put the entry two blocks closer to the action downtown. Making this simple shift, the studio hewed to Fentress' design principle that relies on discovering the natural order of a building and its site.

While making the convention center more a part of city life, Fentress incorporated the existing structure – a move that emulates the expansion of the Colorado Convention Center and repurposes what was a serviceable building. A new unified interior design scheme erased any dilemma caused by the perception of "old" versus "new," while employing a color palette and selection of materials that borrowed from the desert aesthetic.

A site plan of the Palm Springs Convention Center shows the organization of the building.

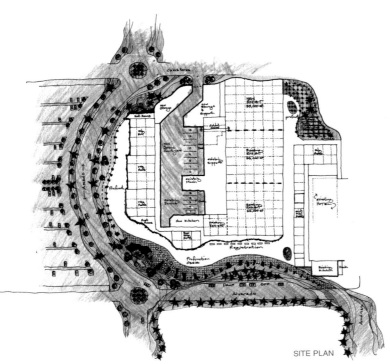

SITE PLAN

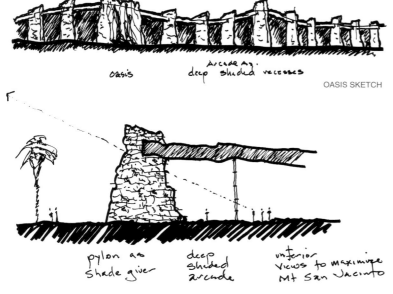

oasis   Arcade Ag.
deep shaded recesses

OASIS SKETCH

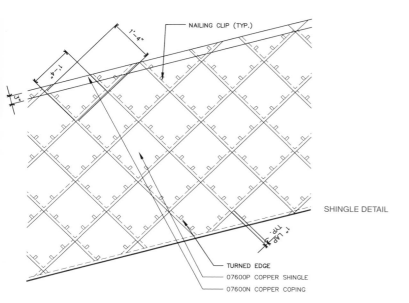

pylon as
shade giver

deep
shaded
arcade

interior
views to maximize
Mt San Jacinto

PYLON SKETCH

NAILING CLIP (TYP.)

SHINGLE DETAIL

TURNED EDGE
07600P COPPER SHINGLE
07600N COPPER COPING

In the meantime, the exterior design reveals a building with an organic and curved sensibility that echoes the dramatic backdrop of the San Jacinto Mountains. The convention center's soaring pylons form a colonnade along the stone façade, capturing the rhythm of the mountains while recalling the peaks' eroding edges. This immersion in context continues in the fascia, a sinuous woven strip of copper that tops the colonnade in a rich, gleaming material. Here, as with the interior motif, the convention center looks to the desert for inspiration.

"That scaled look has a feeling of desert plant materials or snakeskin, the way it overlaps in a diamond pattern," says Winters. "You see that angular form in desert designs. Copper seemed appropriate for Palm Springs." In essence, those entering the convention center will, at once, encounter the meeting of mountains and desert.

Appearance, however, is not everything, especially in a building that requires the flexibility to accommodate numerous types of events. The Palm Springs Convention Center includes 120,000 square feet of continuous exhibition space, a 20,000-square-foot ballroom, and 19 break-out rooms of various sizes.

In a move to link the interior to its setting, Fentress designed an 18,000-square-foot lobby with a panoramic view of the mountains and a connection to an outdoor gathering place. There, water flows over a rock installation, again bringing the natural setting into the city's meeting place.

The importance of allowing natural light into a meeting hall and establishing a connection to surroundings has not been ignored. Though long considered a potential distraction, the generous but controlled use of windows distinguishes Fentress' convention center designs, putting the comfort of visitors on the meeting agenda.

The desert influenced the materials and details used in the convention center arcade. The woven look of the copper fascia on the overhang stems from the patterns found on snakeskins and desert plants. During the design, the studio specifically calculated the sight line to make sure visitors could see the top of the mountains from the interior.

The San Jacinto Mountains inspired the convention center design, including the rolling curves of the entry overhang and the rugged stone pylons. The lobby connects to an outdoor plaza. Changes in light accentuate the texture of the metal fascia and the trees (following spread).

DESERT MODERNISM

Palm Springs has carried on a long love affair with Modernist architecture, with its devotion to openness and the inclusion of outdoor living spaces. Homes by Modernists such as Richard Neutra, John Lautner and Albert Frey inspired the concept of Desert Modernism, which refers to a style that became popular here in the 1930s. By including native materials, liberal glass walls and windows, and open floor plans, architects also succeeded in bringing Palm Springs' much-heralded climate into play every day. The Palm Springs

LOADING ZONE

SANTA FE COMMUNITY CONVENTION CENTER

Location **Santa Fe, New Mexico**
Client **City of Santa Fe**
Year **2008**

Curtis Fentress "It is a building that looks as if it had always been in Santa Fe, where context and culture form the basis of daily life."

For more than a century, creative people have responded to the lure of Santa Fe. It begins with the light, a clear, almost piercingly beautiful light that has captured the heart of artists worldwide. There is the soft brown of the adobe homes, punctuated with bright jolts of turquoise and cobalt and pink, a style that looks to the simplicity of the past. And there is the scale of the city, a low-rise ensemble that is made for walking and sampling Santa Fe's exotic mix of art and regional food.

Santa Fe bills itself as The City Different, and that it is, with a mixture of cultural heritages; Hispanic, Native American and Anglo influences give it a flavor not found anywhere else in the United States.

A project in Santa Fe would seem to be a natural for an architect such as Fentress, who looks to context and culture to guide design and find identity. But this city doesn't leave much to chance in terms of architectural concepts. The unusual conformity of architectural style in much of the city is no accident: in the 1950s, the city passed laws that determined what can be built in the city's historical areas, which include the Plaza and surrounding streets. Anything constructed since that time must have a certain profile, and a look that mirrors or interprets a Pueblo Revival style. The required adobe walls in earth tones and assorted architectural gestures recall rural structures built before Santa Fe adopted a more Eurocentric Territorial design vocabulary. Design review is, in short, a strict taskmaster.

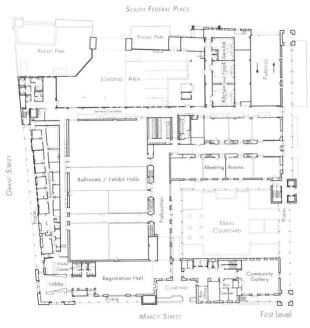

SOUTH FEDERAL PLACE

POCKET PARK

POCKET PARK

LOADING AREA

PARKING

Kitchen and Food Service

Service Corridor

GRANT STREET

Ballrooms / Exhibit Halls

Meeting Rooms

Prefunction

MAIN COURTYARD

PORTAL

PORTAL

Visitor Center

Lobby

Registration Hall

Courtyard

Box Office

Bus Center

Community Gallery

PORTAL

MARCY STREET

First Level

FLOOR PLAN

Translating forms used in small dwellings into larger and more complex public spaces for the Santa Fe Community Convention Center required placing two-level structures to the edge, as shown in plan. The interior is influenced by detailing that is a hallmark of Santa Fe's historic style.

The design was created by employing the best elements of "Santa Fe Style." By studying and understanding this architectural vocabulary and using it wisely, Fentress made this large building program fit into the Santa Fe urban fabric in an integrated and thoughtful manner.

The challenge was finding the best way to accommodate the basic "givens" for a convention center, which is not a humble adobe home. A convention center is big, with a program that calls for a generous exhibition hall, a spacious banquet area, numerous meeting rooms, and, if it is a center by the Fentress studio, generous interior daylighting as well as the creation of links to the outside community.

Crucial here is the idea of finding the natural order – the smart circulation and flow that makes a large, complex building easy for visitors to navigate and that provides flexibility for meeting planners. Strong sustainable practices were imperative in arid Santa Fe, where water is precious and environmental stewardship is expected.

Curtis Fentress says he considered the city's design review process just one of the many requirements any project must meet, whether staying within budget, meeting deadlines, or developing consensus among community groups.

"Working in Santa Fe taught us about the strong blend of cultures and the pride people have in their city. Studying their style of architecture helped us learn how it can be applied to many different types of public buildings."

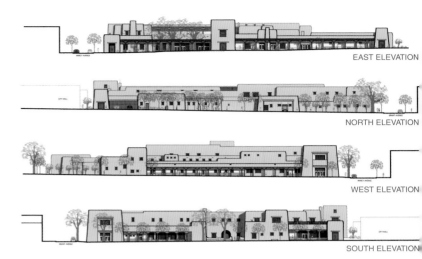

EAST ELEVATION

NORTH ELEVATION

WEST ELEVATION

SOUTH ELEVATION

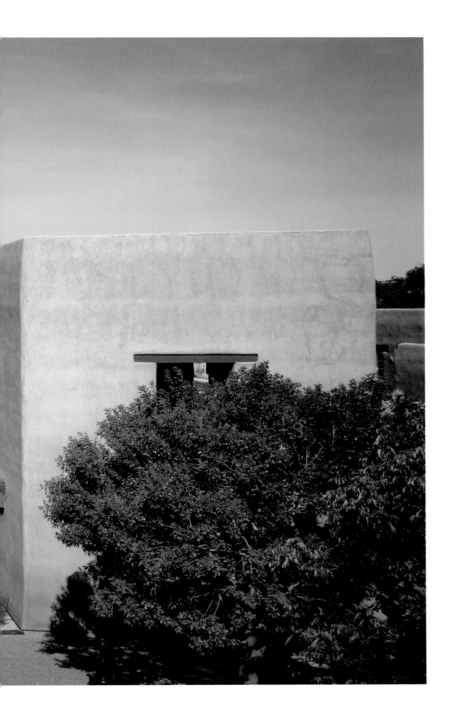

The inclusion of a courtyard and other outdoor gathering spaces lets those attending conferences take a break and enjoy the beauty of New Mexico's sky, while showing diversity of scale as demonstrated in the elevations (above). Many of the exterior wooden elements were crafted of material reclaimed from a nearby forest fire (following spread), a strategy that helped the convention center earn LEED Gold certification.

After years of holding conventions in a former high school gymnasium, officials knew the city needed a gathering place that was larger and more flexible if Santa Fe were to remain popular with visitors. The new convention center holds 9,000 square feet in both meeting and pre-function space, with 20,000 square feet devoted to an exhibition hall and ballroom. Multiple simultaneous events can claim their own exhibition area, break-out rooms, and dining areas. Meeting rooms and exhibition spaces can be used in different configurations. The courtyard and a rooftop terrace link indoors and outdoors.

For the new convention center, Fentress set the larger elements – the expansive exhibition hall and banquet space – toward the center. The studio then surrounded that with low-rise forms to contain more intimate functions, a move that stepped back the mass and reduced the sense of bulk. Rather than tack on stylistic gestures that speak to "Santa Fe Style," such elements were integrated into the design: plentiful wooden forms, practical arcaded walkways known as portales, a courtyard for contemplation or events, and adobe-style walls with rounded edges and earth-tone finishes.

This facility also is knitted into the community as it greets the surrounding streets. It is filled with daylight, and is stringent enough about sustainability in materials and building techniques to have earned LEED Gold certification from the U.S. Green Building Council. This goes beyond the expected approaches to conserving water and energy; for example, the exterior timber used for lintels and corbels is pine reclaimed from a nearby forest fire.

Meanwhile, the interior is marked by design elements that reinforce a sense of place, including wooden beams, fireplaces and carpeting that take their cue from Navajo textiles. Large windows, skylights and clerestories provide natural light, even in interior spaces deep within the convention center.

A city that revels in 400 years of history now has the tools to meet the future: a convention center design with timeless appeal, wrapped around a state-of-the-art core.

THE REAL SANTA FE STYLE?

Christine Mather and Sharon Woods' 1993 book *Santa Fe Style* bubbled over with lush photographs of adobe walls, bold-colored doors, and the architectural gestures such as vigas and portales that distinguish this multi-cultural city.

But the real force behind the term "Santa Fe Style," which forever changed the city's architectural style to one of Pueblo Revival conformity, was Isaac Hamilton Rapp. His designs for prominent downtown buildings such as the 1915 Museum of Fine Arts of the Museum of New Mexico and the 1920 La Fonda hotel, set the standard for the style that city officials in the late 1950s codified as the approved "look" for buildings constructed in Santa Fe's historic districts. Eventually, the city also included the Territorial style in the rule book. In both instances, adobe walls, prominent parapets, and wood detailing helped define architectural expression, making this city look like no place else.

Regionally inspired art, the generous use of warm wood, and places for gathering or rest are gestures throughout the convention center.

LAWRENCE ARGENT

Artist Lawrence Argent paints and works in photo-based imagery, but he is known primarily for his provocative sculptures and installations around the world.

Provocative? For this artist, who was born in England and raised in Australia, the idea is to blur the distinction between high art and low art, dragging art out of the museum or gallery, and setting it down firmly on the street. In the process, his non-hierarchical strategy pulls from representation, conceptualism, humor and a jolt of mischief, all designed to make people examine their surroundings, their intentions and their lives.

Argent is a pioneer in using 3-D technology and nontraditional materials in his work. The same inquisitive spirit drives Curtis Fentress, who always seeks more intelligent and sustainable solutions to problems involving materials, process and design.

He is candid about addressing the role his children have played in the way he approaches the idea of object and subject. The way he looks at things, really. His explorations of form and concept relate to place, culture, and the innate sense of human curiosity, just as designs by Curtis Fentress rely on the context of a project and the relationship of the building to its community, in order to marry building to site.

As Argent says, "Art can become more familiar if we can laugh at it first, then look at the seriousness and reflect on what we're looking at."

With *I See What You Mean* (Big Blue Bear), a 40-foot tall faceted blue bear outside the Colorado Convention Center — the color was what he calls purely "serendipitous" — Argent considered the relationship of locals and visitors, as well as the stereotypical view many out-of-towners have of Colorado. Just as many area residents will never spend a minute in the convention center, this Big Blue Bear is curious to know just what all these strangers are doing in there.

The techniques Argent used were groundbreaking. His model for the bear was created through the use of a rapid prototyping machine, a printing device that turns digital images into dimensional objects. Argent then worked with the computer animation and visual effects production company Pixel Kitchen, of Boulder, Colorado, to create hundreds of thousands of triangulations in the bear's image to expand the figure into a 40-foot-tall bear.

From there, the process shifted to Kreysler and Associates of American Canyon, California, where Argent machined segments of the surface from blocks of disposable, recyclable foam. These created molds for the bear's fiberglass "skin." Segment by segment — up to about 70 in all — led to the full exterior shell of the sculpture. A steel skeleton, or armature, fills about one-third of the piece, and segments were assembled like a big dimensional jigsaw puzzle. Bulkheads were installed at strategic spots to strengthen the sculpture as segments were joined. The sculpture was shipped to Denver in five pieces, and erected on the Colorado Convention Center site on a very windy day.

"Obviously, no one entity can possess all the accoutrements to define all of Colorado, but there are icons that are used profusely for this relationship. With a tongue-in-cheek approach, I thought about the fauna being representative of the mountains. The type of fauna merged as an image of the bear, and more specifically, the black bear. The image of the bear has been transformed into chainsaw-sculpted personages or somewhat realistic representations that confer a 'regional Western art' aesthetic. Reinforcing my mission of public art being the ability to communicate a non-hierarchical art experience that can be interpreted on many levels, the element of whimsy became augmented when I wished to make it really large."

As for *Untitled* (The Red Rabbit), in Terminal B of Sacramento International Airport, Argent says he has no wish to become an "animal" artist, despite the fact that one of his most talked-about works is a big blue bear and his portfolio of public art commissions soon will include a big red rabbit. But the concept of dramatizing the anxiety travelers feel hovering around a baggage carousel waiting for their belongings to pop out of the chute was just too strong to ignore.

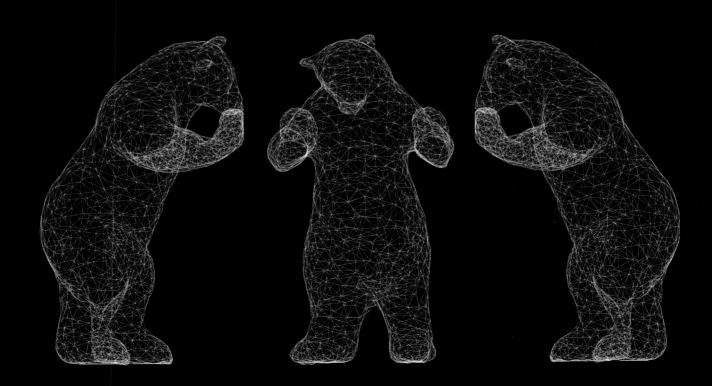

"What surfaced repeatedly as I looked into what I was attempting to create to interact with the space emerged from the amplified meaning associated with 'baggage,' literally and metaphorically," Argent says. "The joy in the sense of reconciliation, the part that was separated is now joined, to form the happy union of owner and owned. It is spit out on the rotating tarmac; yes, it's yours, the elation, relief, the ode to now being complete after the 'journey.' You feel one again."

The untitled, three-part sculptural installation for the University of Houston includes three orbs – two of stone and one of bronze. Argent used computer modeling and prototyping equipment to design the markings for the pieces. He then transmitted the digitized data to a fabricator in China for the raw materials to be carved by hand.

"The human element is where things change, where mistakes can be made, so that these pieces are not perfect. You look at the work and you say 'You've got it, but something about it is different.' "

Head of the sculpture department at the University of Denver, Lawrence Argent trained in sculpture at the Royal Melbourne Institute of Technology in Australia and earned a Master of Fine Arts degree from the Rinehart School of Sculpture at the Maryland Institute, College of Art, in Baltimore. He has received numerous fellowships and been an artist-in-residence at the John Michael Kohler Foundation. He has made his home in Denver since the early 1990s, moving here to teach at DU.

Argent was playing with his children and a veritable zoo of stuffed animals when the idea clicked for the sculpture outside the Colorado Convention Center. He asked himself, "which was the most potent one" in terms of the animal's pull on memory and emotion. The bear won. "Life and Art have always intertwined themselves in peculiar ways for me...Over recent years my domestic landscape has altered considerably. I have two young children that in perpetuity litter my terrain with new forms, some recognizable and others not so.

"As I lay there with the side of my face imprinted with the fine weaving of the living room carpet from my much-needed catatonic slumber, I crank open my eyelids to a new vista. It is here I began looking afresh at these pieces of plastic, wood, rubber and fur alongside my assumptions of my children's own possible perception and association. As I was decoding their language of materiality and form and removing subjectivity from this digestion, it became apparent my journey was to play with how something, 'an object,' once de-contextualized has potential for unnerving the familiar."

3 MUSEUMS

NATIONAL MUSEUM OF THE MARINE CORPS
NATIONAL COWBOY AND WESTERN HERITAGE
NATIONAL MUSEUM OF WILDLIFE ART
MUSEUM OF SCIENCE | BOSTON

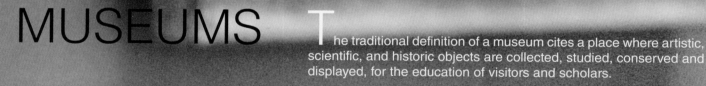

MUSEUMS

The traditional definition of a museum cites a place where artistic, scientific, and historic objects are collected, studied, conserved and displayed, for the education of visitors and scholars.

How stuffy that seems compared to the way a museum can affect our lives.

A museum promises learning and excitement. As we near the entry, we feel the anticipation, the realization that knowledge, beauty and experience wait inside. As we walk from gallery to gallery, stop for a snack, or purchase a book, we follow a path that leads to recognition, of our world, our location, ourselves. The art can soothe, prod, even confound. The scientific discoveries can amaze and instruct. And the history: we learn where we have been, all the better to understand where we might be going.

This marriage of context, culture, and community comes together in harmony in projects that are the ideal vehicle for a sense of wonder, and that is a key part of how Fentress identifies the design of a museum. As with all public buildings, museums must be easy to navigate, while offering surprise and delight. These are places that take us out of the ordinary and deposit us into the realm of the heart, the mind and the soul.

The National Museum of the Marine Corps, for instance, is a repository for historical artifacts and information regarding the Corps, which was founded in 1775 but remains a living, breathing community of one. The Corps' iconic emblem, a 1945 photograph of the flag-raising at Iwo Jima, inspired Fentress to make the focal point an angular skylight that signals more than just the museum's allegiance. This symbolic gesture also beckons visitors and floods the interior with daylight. Inside, there is peace, won through bravery.

The National Museum of Wildlife Art has a much more subtle presence, so quiet that its rough stone walls appear to merge into the butte on which the building stands. A now-you-see-it, now-you-don't approach stokes a sense of intrigue, while the scenic surroundings and wildlife serve as a prep course for the art displayed inside. This link between nature and culture amplifies pleasure, but also adds layers of understanding to what hangs on the walls.

For those who revel in the myth and reality of the West, the National Cowboy and Western Heritage Museum is all about time travel, though there are still working cowboys. The long history of the cowboy in many cultural guises suffuses this institution, which Fentress made much more interesting to explore.

All museums teach, in terms of their collections, exhibitions and programming. But the successful science museum teaches by example. Such is the case with the Museum of Science in Boston, a premier institution in the field of environmental education, and sustainable practices and theory. Fentress' master plan and Gordon Wing happily accepted the charge from officials: use the new building to demonstrate materials and strategies to people from all walks of life. Test concepts, be innovative, and make clear that this is a guide for those who want to keep planet Earth a healthy home.

For a museum to be honest with visitors – about duty and service, about our wildlife, about our national identity, and about our world and its future – the place must be honest in itself, where drama is the byproduct of enriching contents, intent and design. The container must respect the contents, not overwhelm or consume, so that building and objects work together. And where visitors can hardly wait to come back to learn something new.

NATIONAL MUSEUM OF THE MARINE CORPS

Location **Quantico, Virginia**
Owner **Marine Corps Heritage Foundation**
Year **2006**

Curtis Fentress "The National Museum of the Marine Corps, to me, is all about peace and peacekeeping. It was a daunting responsibility and a great challenge to create an icon for a group that has bonded through a shared culture."

1

Almost 30 years ago, the United States Congress appropriated money so each branch of the country's armed forces could build a national museum. For the Marine Corps Heritage Foundation, the Marine Corps, and the Naval Facilities Command, the real task was to find an architecture firm that could "get it," with a design that could embody, in bricks and mortar, what it means to be a Marine.

It took thought and time: Officials announced the competition in late 2000. From an initial field of more than 30 architects, four finalists emerged. In July 2001, Fentress won first prize and began the studio's full engagement to design the National Museum of the Marine Corps, the heart of the 135-acre Marine Corps Heritage Center at the Marine Corps Base Quantico.

The studio's homework paid off: an intense immersion in the culture of the Corps, its traditions, and legendary courage in tough situations. Reading about the Marines, talking to Marines, watching documentaries on Marines, and dissecting Hollywood's gauzy portrayal of Marines, the Fentress studio sought a symbol that in the blink of an eye summed up the Corps' long, proud history.

The answer lay in a photograph that captured a moment of teamwork and heroism in the face of death.

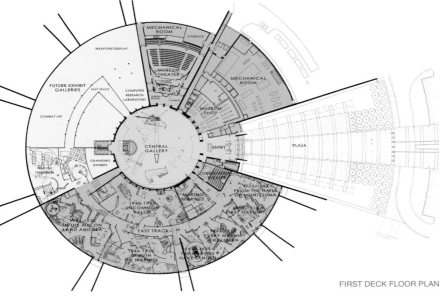

FIRST DECK FLOOR PLAN

The National Museum of the Marine Corps celebrates its entry, welcoming visitors to explore the history of the Corps. The atrium forms a natural core for galleries and visitor amenities (plan, left).

The canted skylight and mast recall the angle of the flagpole being raised by Marines on Iwo Jima in Joe Rosenthal's iconic photograph (following spread).

"That image – Joe Rosenthal's 1945 photograph of six Marines planting a flag on Mount Suribachi in Iwo Jima – rejuvenated our country," says Curtis Fentress. "My father told me this when I was a kid. I saw that photograph, and asked, 'What is that?' and he said, 'These guys, these Marines, they planted that flag on a mountain and pushed the Japanese off of there.' He said that during the war, this image of the men in this photograph turned the whole country around."

From the angle of that long-ago flagpole being raised, Fentress distilled a central feature for the museum: a 210-foot steel mast that anchors the entry lobby and supports a ribbed, conical skylight. The mast is a signature element of the building, a low-slung, circular concrete structure partially covered by earthen berms. In the soaring travertine-lined core space, aircraft are suspended from the beams, and ground vehicles seem to prowl a terrazzo floor poured in an earth-meets-sea design. Ringing this central gallery on the first floor is space to display multimedia and interactive exhibitions; upstairs is reserved for classrooms, offices, art galleries, and two restaurants.

"The vegetated roof of the museum is just one of the many strategies Fentress used to create a sustainable project," says principal Brian Chaffee. "The skylight's glass panels are high-performance, tinted, low-emissivity, insulated and laminated, both to save energy and conserve the artifacts inside."

The completion of the museum signaled the end of the first phase of a master plan that calls for the continuing build-out of Semper Fidelis Memorial Park, expansion of the museum to complete the exhibition space, and the addition of other community elements. In October 2009, Fentress' small, rustic Semper Fidelis Memorial Chapel opened, a contemporary interpretation of a field chapel built of wood and stone.

Together, museum and chapel form a compelling ensemble that speaks to the Corps' history as well as individual aspiration. For the head of the Marine Corps Heritage Foundation, the key is the architect's commitment to client and culture, a crucial requirement for architects during the design competiton.

"Curt Fentress is an exceptional and exemplary architect who understands how to listen, learn and be inspired by history, culture, people and places," says Lieutenant General Ron Christmas. "From this understanding, he creates designs that are inspiring and timeless."

Fentress also understands the importance of perseverance.

"In war and in design, we need to be patient," says Fentress. "It's one hill at a time."

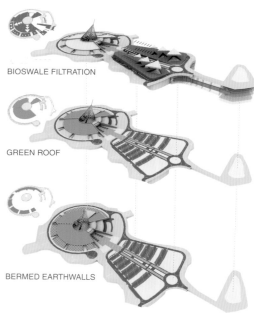

BIOSWALE FILTRATION

GREEN ROOF

BERMED EARTHWALLS

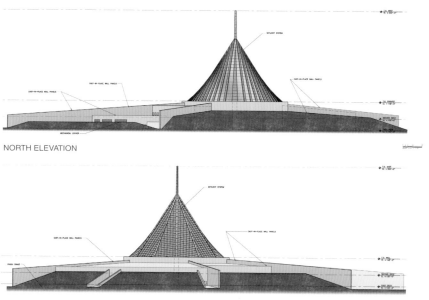

NORTH ELEVATION

SOUTH ELEVATION

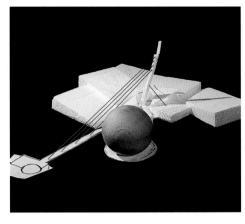

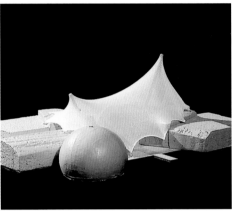

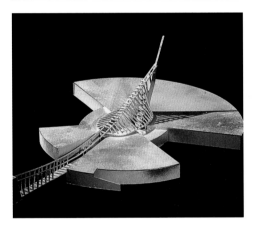

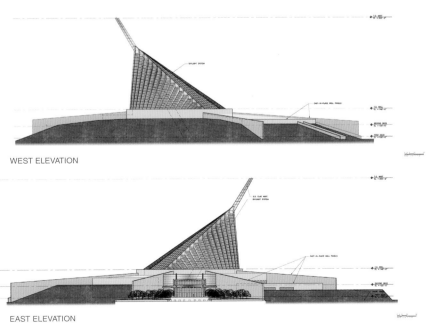

WEST ELEVATION

EAST ELEVATION

Design development addresses many issues. The process of identifying smart and sustainable practices was key for the museum (far left), while elevations capturing directional views pinpoint the placement of the mast and skylight (left).

The evolution of the museum massing and form settled on a circular building topped by an innovative identifying element (above).

The museum's atrium does more than orient visitors; it also serves as a ceremonial space for events, such as commissioning new officers or bestowing medals (above). Exhibitions include artwork, interactive displays, and aircraft and other vehicles used by the Corps.

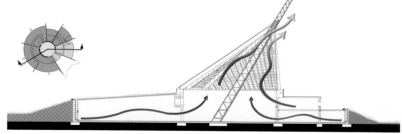

SECTION DIAGRAM

Among the 8,000 pieces in the Marine Corps Combat Art Collection is the James Montgomery Flagg (1877-1960) oil on canvas *First in the Fight*, commissioned by the Marine Corps to be used as a recruiting poster in World War I (above). Experiential galleries give visitors a chance to briefly immerse themselves in the life of a Marine.

The skylight of the museum becomes a beacon along heavily traveled Interstate 95, heading north to Washington, D.C. (following spread).

A PLACE FOR PEACE

When the National Museum of the Marine Corps opened in 2006, it chose the Corps' birthday – November 10 – for the festivities. When the museum expanded its exhibition space in 2010, it selected a day in June to mark a key Allied assault during the long, bloody and decisive Battle for Belleau Wood, in 1918 near Paris. During the successful struggle to push back German forces, more than 1,800 Marines – almost 10,000 Americans in all – died during a conflict that lasted more than three weeks. The three new galleries recount Marine history from its founding in 1775 to 1865, from the post-Civil War years to 1916, and to the years of American involvement in World War I, 1917-1918.

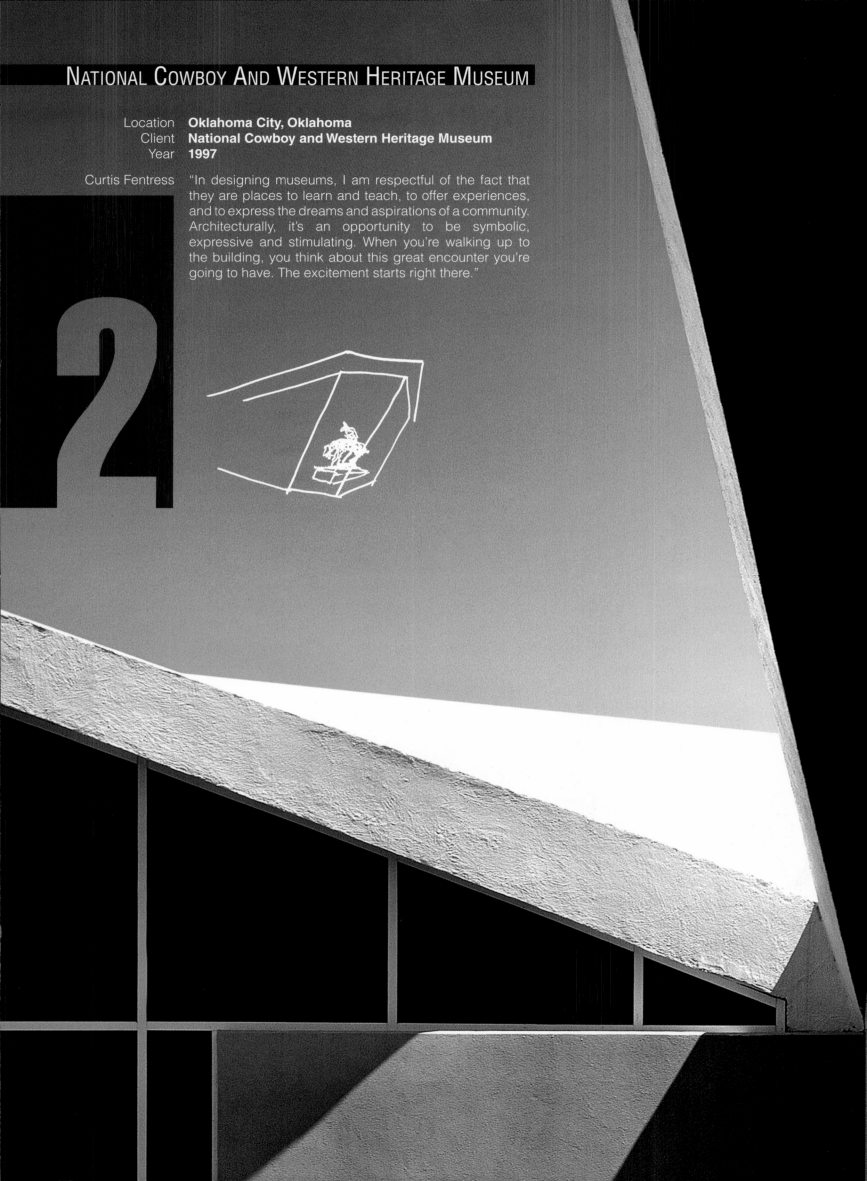

NATIONAL COWBOY AND WESTERN HERITAGE MUSEUM

Location	**Oklahoma City, Oklahoma**
Client	**National Cowboy and Western Heritage Museum**
Year	**1997**

Curtis Fentress — "In designing museums, I am respectful of the fact that they are places to learn and teach, to offer experiences, and to express the dreams and aspirations of a community. Architecturally, it's an opportunity to be symbolic, expressive and stimulating. When you're walking up to the building, you think about this great encounter you're going to have. The excitement starts right there."

2

The National Cowboy and Western Heritage Museum has put its own brand on the world of cultural institutions. Its subject is the working cowboy, from the Civil War era to today, and its mission is to collect, preserve and interpret objects of all sorts that refer to this archetypal inhabitant of the American West.

The museum, founded in 1955 in Oklahoma City by a group of art and history lovers representing more than a dozen Western states, needed more room and better organization to showcase its collections, events and experiences, including an unusual – and sizeable – replica of an Old West town.

When Fentress won first prize to design a new museum expansion and renovation, the entry of the existing building was difficult to find, and much of the artwork was exposed to daylight from exterior windows. The popular Prosperity Junction, with its "railroad depot" and "pioneer church," was in the basement. Since the building lacked an elevator, it was difficult for many visitors to reach all of the exhibitions.

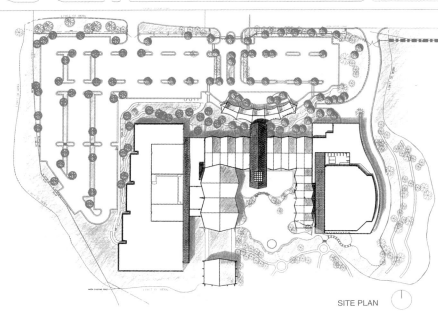

The site plan of the National Cowboy and Western Heritage Museum indicates placement of the new canopy entrance and the new building devoted to galleries. The older building is now used for visitor services.

SITE PLAN

"The old building had reached the end of the trail," says Curtis Fentress, referring to the once-state-of-the-art structure with a thin-shell folded-plate concrete roof. "We used the existing space for the gift shop, meeting and seminar rooms – areas that could operate with daylight – and we inserted a new dramatic entrance. We celebrated the entry with a canopy that shaded and welcomed visitors, making it easy to find and understand. New expansive wings on either side as bookends offered more space for exhibitions and a great hall and ballroom for events. Children have their own area now, and the gardens are inviting for everyone."

Museum officials wanted to be responsible stewards, and set about to raise money for a gradual expansion that eventually took almost a decade to complete. Fentress worked closely with staff to devise a master plan that allowed the project to become reality, adding space after space, while the museum was operational and stayed open the entire time.

To immerse visitors in the Western experience, Fentress drew upon historic imagery for perhaps the most dramatic exhibition area, designed to showcase one of the museum's prize holdings: James Earle Fraser's poignant *End of the Trail*. The glass-walled corridor with a soaring, canted roof recalls the thrust of a prairie schooner, the covered wagon that brought thousands of settlers west to a new life. There stands the massive plaster version of Fraser's sculpture, which he made for display at the 1915 Panama-Pacific International Exposition in San Francisco. The museum acquired the piece in the late 1960s, restored it, and in exchange created a bronze casting of the sculpture for the California park where the plaster work had found a home. Yet this initial focal point, this nod to the Native Americans' loss of land, is just the tip of the museum's extensive collection and displays, which attract more than 200,000 visitors each year.

Fraser's *End of the Trail* became an icon of the 163,000-square-foot expansion and renovation of the original 77,000-square-foot two-level building. But the history of the museum lives in a sun-splashed corridor, where busts of the original founders were put on view, after years in storage. They join a larger sculpture: the governor of Oklahoma. In 1956, Oklahoma Governor Raymond Gary helped win over representatives from Western states haggling over placing the museum in more than 40 cities. It's possible to imagine the horse-trading that went on at those meetings, but eventually they settled on Oklahoma City, corralling the museum for the Sooner State.

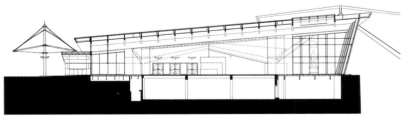

LONGITUDINAL SECTION

The original museum building, in background, sets off a pavilion inspired by the thrust of a Prairie Schooner, the wagon that brought many people to Oklahoma and the West.

SECTION

The pavilion in which James Earle Fraser's *End of the Trail* is installed offers a singular visitor experience, but is visible throughout the museum. Busts of founders of the museum line a sun-splashed corridor, taking a place of honor (facing page).

END OF THE TRAIL

American artist James Earle Fraser (1876-1953) parlayed a talent for sculpture into studies at the Ecole des Beaux-Arts in Paris, later working with noted artist Augustus Saint-Gaudens. Fraser became known for his portrait sculptures, his carvings for coins (including the American Indian Head nickel), and monumental pieces, including *End of the Trail*, which became a symbol of Native Americans being forced into a restricted life and a fight to preserve their cultures. Fraser, who had befriended Native Americans during his boyhood on the Plains, made a small model of *Trail* that earned him international attention. He created the 17-foot-tall plaster cast for the 1915 Panama-Pacific International Exposition in San Francisco, California, but material shortages during World War I made it impossible to cast the piece in bronze.

At the end of the exposition, the cast was discarded. People who lived in Tulare County, California, salvaged it, and installed it at a nearby park. In 1968, the National Cowboy & Western Heritage Museum made a smart trade: officials acquired the plaster work, cast it in bronze, sent the metal sculpture back to California, and gave the plaster version a place of prominence in the museum. Fraser's small maquette of the work is on loan to the Denver Art Museum for exhibition.

NATIONAL MUSEUM OF WILDLIFE ART

Location	**Jackson, Wyoming**
Client	**National Museum of Wildlife Art**
Year	**1994**

Curtis Fentress "Wyoming is breathtakingly dramatic, heart-achingly beautiful. From the road, the museum looks more like a ruin. You see the bands of color in the butte. You see the stone. It has different effects on different people. But they get it. In designing this museum, we were mindful not to compete, but to complement, nature's work."

Some buildings never seem to belong, no matter how carefully they are designed.

But others feel as if they have always been there.

Crafted of field stone in a series of planar and organic shapes, the National Museum of Wildlife Art sits on a plateau on the East Gros Ventre Butte. It is across from the Jackson National Elk Refuge, above a Wyoming valley marked by the singular beauty of the surrounding mountains. Years earlier, the site had been terraced to provide spaces for workforce housing and, later, a campground. Then the site sat abandoned and scarred.

Enter the board of the National Wildlife Art Museum in Jackson Hole. Members faced a big decision and chose the path of great opportunity: to move the museum to the new site, giving the facility more prominence and space, while allowing it to showcase wildlife art in a place surrounded by many of those same creatures. Here, nature and culture could merge.

The museum, founded in the mid-1980s, had been housed in a small commercial storefront on Jackson Hole's Town Square. On one hand, the location attracted a captive downtown audience. But it did not support the museum's mission for growth.

ELEVATION

Viewed from below, the walls of the National Museum of Wildlife Art suggest the ruin of a prehistoric structure rather than a contemporary place of learning, as detailed in this elevation.

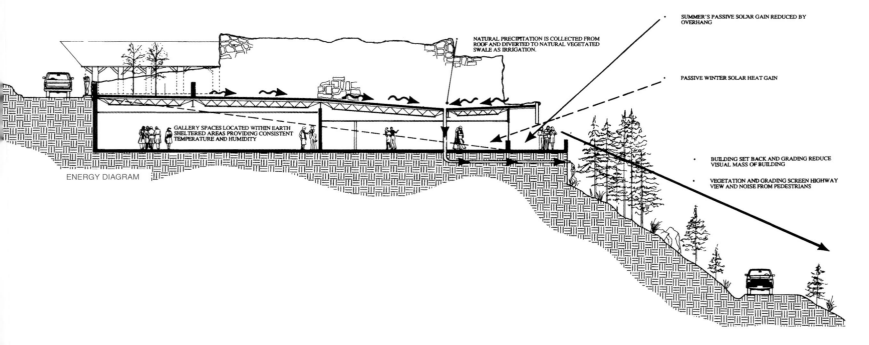

SUMMER'S PASSIVE SOLAR GAIN REDUCED BY OVERHANG

NATURAL PRECIPITATION IS COLLECTED FROM ROOF AND DIVERTED TO NATURAL VEGETATED SWALE AS IRRIGATION.

PASSIVE WINTER SOLAR HEAT GAIN

GALLERY SPACES LOCATED WITHIN EARTH SHELTERED AREAS PROVIDING CONSISTENT TEMPERATURE AND HUMIDITY

ENERGY DIAGRAM

BUILDING SET BACK AND GRADING REDUCE VISUAL MASS OF BUILDING

VEGETATION AND GRADING SCREEN HIGHWAY VIEW AND NOISE FROM PEDESTRIANS

Fentress reclaimed 23 acres of damaged land for the museum site, grading it back to its original contour. Tucking the museum into the butte showed respect for the land forms. Logs used in the entry were repurposed from the site. The beauty of Wyoming sets the tone, as nature and culture merge in this courtyard (facing page).

Soon after Fentress won first prize in a national design competition. the studio reclaimed 23 acres, graded the land back to its original contour, and added topsoil in order to plant indigenous materials that encouraged wildlife to return there.

The museum's entry faces away from the highway below the building, which is reached through a dramatic drive up the butte.

"You get a sense of discovery," says Curtis Fentress. "You approach the building. You see it. You come off the highway. And it has this baroque kind of entry. You just see a rock wall. Then you swing around a big curve and more of the museum is unveiled. You come to the log entry. The main body of the museum is built into the hillside. The rock wall merges into this entrance.

"The museum sits on one of the plateaus, the parking on the other," he continued. "We were conscientious about preserving the environment for both the wildlife and the art. We celebrated the entry while stressing sustainability by building it from wood salvaged from the site."

For all its sense of melting into the land, the museum is a museum. Years of experience working on gallery and museum design gave Fentress the skills to bring smart organization to the interior, allowing the 35,000-square-foot building to showcase its collection, while boosting its attendance from 5,000 people a year to more than 80,000.

The canyon-like lobby offers framed views of the elk refuge. Visitors then enter galleries for traveling exhibitions and shows built around the more than 5,000 objects in the museum's collection of paintings, sculpture and works on paper, with work by important artists as diverse as George Catlin, Edward Hicks, Allan Houser, Carl Rungius and John Nieto. The complex also offers generous space for community events, research and scholarship, a film series, and programs on art and wildlife. A café and exterior terrace afford stunning views, while offering visitors a chance to relax, soak in the beauty of the site, and watch the elk roam free in the valley.

What may look like a ruin to some is really a vibrant arts center, where striking vistas, a responsive building and dynamic art exist as one. Through careful planning and sensitive contextual references, the wildlife art museum blends the art inside with some of the country's most beautiful scenery.

Galleries filled with nature's bounty lead off an entry where wild animal "footprints" create directional tracks (top right).

Canada-based artist Robert Bateman captured the spirit of the bison in his 1997 acrylic on canvas, *Chief.* Robert Bateman© (right).

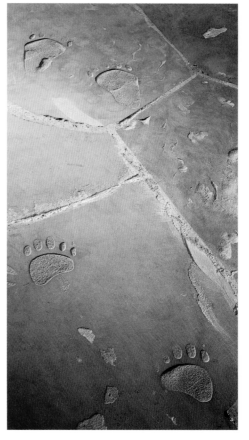

RETURN OF THE NATIVE

The stunning setting of the National Museum of Wildlife Art – the National Elk Refuge – was created in 1912 because the elk herd in Jackson, Wyoming, was dying of starvation. First settled in the early 1800s as a trapping and trading center, Jackson Hole was virtually abandoned 40 years later. But as settlers moved west, newly minted national parks began attracting tourists, and when winters turned harsh, the native elk were losing habitat on which to feed. The refuge is administered by the U.S. Fish & Wildlife Service and covers almost 25,000 acres for winter range, about 25 percent of the original land mass used by elk there for centuries.

Another animal symbolic of the American West, the bison, was in a more desperate place. From herds of bison roaming the plains, hundreds of thousands strong, the count by the end of the nineteenth century had dwindled to a handful. Overhunted for food and fur, the American buffalo was considered an endangered species. Conservationists began to bring the breed back through careful management. As a result, Robert Bateman's powerful painting *Chief*, along with other representations of the bison in the National Museum of Wildlife Art, is a celebration, not a souvenir.

MUSEUM OF SCIENCE | BOSTON

Location **Boston, Massachusetts**
Client **Museum of Science, Boston**
Year **Phase 1: 2007**

Curtis Fentress "Let's create a museum that will say *science* for the next decade, maybe even the next century."

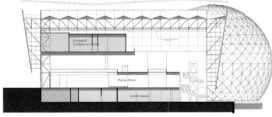

The generous use of glass allows daylighting to cut energy costs, part of the architectural strategy for a building that is a demonstration project for sustainable practices and materials.

The glass-clad planetarium is designed to glow at night, a beacon on the skyline. The museum program calls for separate entries to handle visitors to different functions.

F or 180 years, the Museum of Science in Boston has devoted itself to informing the community about natural history and the sciences. It started as a Back Bay gathering place where Bostonians enamored with science could store the specimens they collected around the world, and evolved into a noted institution that seeks to transform the nation's relationship with science and technology.

The current museum site straddles the Charles River Basin, with one foot in the city of Boston and the other in the city of Cambridge. Over the years, the facility has grown organically, as new structures have been added for exhibitions, research and education. But officials wanted to develop a more powerful profile for the museum, increasing its popularity with regional residents and visitors while expanding its role as a thought leader in the field of science education.

Officials recognized a need to refine circulation, in a sense discovering the natural order within the museum and creating a flow that was more intuitive for visitors, including those whose destinations were museum offices, research areas, or exhibition spaces.

What the Museum of Science sought was a building that in itself was a teacher, a facility that could inform visitors of all ages about issues ranging from fast-changing technology to core sciences, conserving resources, and promoting a healthy environment – inside and out. It sponsored an international design competition to find an architect who could optimally marry function to aesthetics in a complicated

building. Fentress won the competition, partially because of the studio's "impressive reputation for designing buildings with a strong sense of purpose and place," said museum president Ioannis Miaoulis.

Throughout the plan, the latest advances in science, technology and sustainability are to be introduced into the architecture and interactive exhibits that present the museum as a demonstration project that practices what it preaches.

"If we need a glass wall, let's build a glass wall that shows sustainability in action," says principal Bob Louden. "After more than 60 years, the museum looked like a tired hospital, not a science museum. We focused on how it can be exciting, a place you want to go."

Museum officials and architects ran into the nation's economic slowdown, mandating that the plan be implemented in phases so fund-raising could parallel expansion and renovation.

The first phase of the massive expansion and renovation has been completed: construction of the spacious Gordon Wing, the new

two-level headquarters of the National Center for Technological Literacy and ground zero for the museum's exhibition and research teams. The wing houses a dramatic two-level space with sixty 10-foot-high windows, mezzanine offices, and innovative green elements. Daylighting is accentuated, and the museum notes that environmentally mindful elements cut the wing's energy consumption by 38 percent and energy costs by 33 percent, relative to code. High-performance glass windows feature the use of Nanogel®, a super-insulator applied between glass panes. During demolition, plans call for recycling more than 90 percent of the debris, and water-saving fixtures are to be used throughout.

The overall plan is to be bold and clean, emphasizing honest materials; simple, clear circulation, and a memorable design that works well as a science museum.

"Museum officials said that when they turned on the TV at night to watch the news on *Nightline*, they didn't want to see the John Hancock Tower in Back Bay," says Curtis Fentress. "They wanted to see people standing in front of the science museum. To me that says, 'Give me an image that is spectacular, strong, and uniquely Boston.'"

A sinuous walkway links the elements of the museum to the Charles River. Part of the museum building is sited in Boston, part in Cambridge (above).

Vignettes of design concepts spring from the goals of integrating technology into programs and exhibits, expanding outreach, and renovating existing galleries to improve the overall visitor experience (right).

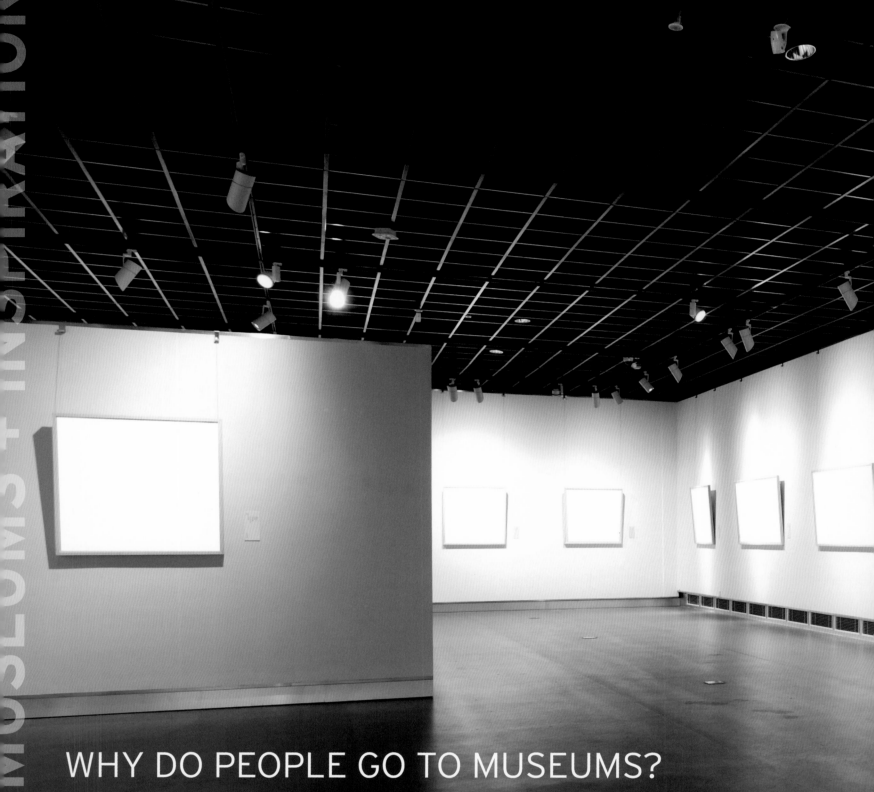

WHY DO PEOPLE GO TO MUSEUMS?

For each person, there is a reason. It can be education, a love of art, the chance to reflect, the need for solitude, stimulation, challenge, fun, shopping, brunch, a place to meet friends, or just something to do on vacation to learn about an unfamiliar city.

Architects must consider all the reasons people visit a museum, as well as preservation of the collection, easy navigation, and community pride.

Design is concerned with context. What is the cultural, artistic, or physical environment of a place? What is its purpose – aesthetic, educational, contemplative? These questions are all explored through architecture for museums. These buildings must be crafted with careful attention to the space and how it will be used. A museum must be adapted to changing exhibitions, and reflect the overall intention.

Within the museum, exhibitions mimic the architectural process – development, schematic design, contract, fabrication and installation. Very often, the production of an art exhibition mirrors the very process of its building. The art it will house, the objects it will display, and the audiences it will attract are of crucial importance in the design of a museum. Who is the museum trying to reach, and what is it trying to present? A successful space considers all of these factors in the design of a building. It is firmly rooted in its surroundings and context.

Fundamentally, the purpose of a museum is to present objects of great cultural and historical value to the public in a setting carefully controlled by curators, conservators, historians and exhibition designers. A team of professionals determines the contents of a museum – and very often the patrons, supporters and donors are instrumental in this process. It is a balance,

a delicate dance to create a museum. As such, the space must be conducive to contemplation, education, and excitement.

Fentress' design for the National Museum of Wildlife Art plants itself firmly within its surroundings. The museum echoes the natural beauty of Jackson, Wyoming, crafted from organic shapes of field stone. Due to the nature of the museum – dedication to the preservation of wildlife – the space is placed at the interesting intersection of culture and nature. A design that takes into account its physical context succeeds in melding the two. Buildings rooted in their natural environment and surroundings create harmony. The National Museum of Wildlife Art is a great example of such design.

A museum also exhibits the importance of education, research and community as fundamental aspects of its work. Though it espouses beauty and aesthetics, a museum is not meant to be a cold place. A sense of involvement and participation for viewers is necessary. People visit museums to engage with the objects, to understand, and to learn – they don't want to feel isolated from what they are seeing.

Another such project that represents the crucial element of education is the National Cowboy and Western Heritage Museum. It houses the ultimate archetype of the American West – the cowboy – and traces its history throughout time and space. This space was reinvented and updated to create a building that allows visitors to understand the Western experience.

Internationally renowned and well-known museums – the Louvre in Paris, the Metropolitan Museum of Art in New York, the British Museum of Art, the National Palace Museum in Taipei, the Uffizi in Florence, and others – house the most important works of art and culture in the world. They boast collections that are intimately tied to the commerce of the art world. Pieces of art become prized possessions of each city. Museums become emblematic of a city, and the culture that it values.

Sometimes, however, a museum is meant to honor an ideology or a group of people. Fentress' National Museum of the Marine Corps pays homage to servicemen and women, and attempts to display what it means to be a Marine. The iconic image shot by Joe Rosenthal of Marines planting a flag on Mount Suribachi informed Fentress' design in the creation of a steel mast. As a signature element of the building, this evokes the Marines' rich history and shows respect to their service.

Museums are of infinite value to a society. The role of an architect in designing a museum is not unlike the role of a curator. Both must carefully study their subject, select the right materials, and organize space to inform, intrigue and inspire.

The centuries-old sections of what is now known as the Musée de Louvre were reorganized and given a new pyramidal entrance by Pei Cobb Freed & Partners. The entry and skylights opened in 1989, the first phase of their work on the legendary French museum and long-time palace.

4

COMMERCIAL

INVESCO FIELD AT MILE HIGH
WATERMARK LUXURY RESIDENCES
ARRAYA TOWER
1999 BROADWAY
BELL TOWER
DUBAI TOWERS

COMMERCIAL   P

ublic architecture wears many hats, most of them designed to bestow civic identity on a place while helping to unify a community.

With flair and occasional full-blown glitz, it is the commercial project that can put a place on the map. When the building boom in the Middle East made architecture a spectator sport, it was the glittering towers that became instant landmarks. Soaring higher and higher, these mega-buildings aimed for the stars, and stardom.

The Fentress studio grew up on commercial buildings. Curtis Fentress came to Denver in the late 1970s because of a commercial project for Kohn Pedersen Fox. That tower, on a site that helps connect conflicting city grids, has gone through its share of name changes. Fentress, though, stayed, making Denver his home because of its people and healthy lifestyle.

One of the largest challenges soon delivered one of the biggest payoffs: 1999 Broadway, which opened in 1984, sits on what was a rare bit of open land in downtown. Or, almost open. The site holds an historic church, an architectural gem known for its service to people from all walks of life. In designing 1999 Broadway, Fentress studied the site and the church for a design gesture that would deliver a building that showed respect while fulfilling the developer's

investment objectives. The resulting arithmetic spiral and concave façade embraced the church, showcasing its beauty while enlivening that part of the city.

More than two decades later, Fentress crossed the ocean to build several towers in the Middle East, where the words "design" and "competition" have become linked in a new definition. The Arraya Tower, in Kuwait City, Kuwait, is part of an upscale complex that includes retail, office space and a hotel. For this 60-story tower, Fentress sought a slender profile, achieved through pairing complementary design schemes to relate to surrounding buildings. In the process, he designed the fourth-tallest building completed in 2009. The studio then set its sights on Dubai, where a pair of sinuous, almost kinetic towers, dubbed the Dancing Sisters, found inspiration in the country's spice trade and long tradition of folk dance.

Back in Denver, the studio that had given the city an airport and a convention center was offered the opportunity to design a football stadium, a futuristic steel and brick bowl that found a proud place on the skyline and a home within a park-like setting. INVESCO Field at Mile High was not just a replacement for the old Mile High Stadium; it was a transformation in terms of amenities, access and community

Although the studio has designed several residential towers, the Watermark Luxury Residences offered the chance to locate a new ensemble of flats, townhouses and penthouses in one of Denver's oldest neighborhoods on a site that included a grand historic home. Architectural cues from the area's large concentration of Queen Anne dwellings inform a building that brings a contemporary oasis into a dense urban setting.

On the boards is a design for a high-rise apartment tower built primarily of glass. Bell Tower, planned for a key site downtown, will bring a shimmering jolt to the Denver skyline. Double-height suites with oversized balconies will produce backyards in the sky, with unparalleled views – and no mowing. On the edge of the historic district where Denver began in the late 1850s, Bell Tower will signal a new age for the city in terms of forward-thinking design.

INVESCO FIELD AT MILE HIGH

Location **Denver, Colorado**
Client **The Metropolitan Football Stadium District**
Year **2001**

Curtis Fentress "This stadium was designed to get the fans as close as possible to the field."

1

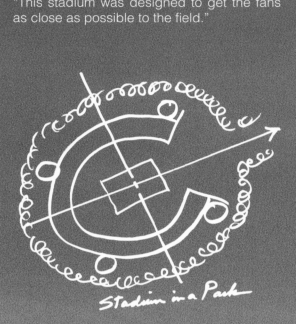

Stadium in a Park

Football is all about the fans, and respecting their experience at games was a goal when the Denver Broncos won voter approval to build a new stadium. As a bonus, Fentress gave the team, the fans and the community a stadium situated in a park, a respite in a dense urban part of the city.

Broncos fans may have felt at home in the old Mile High Stadium, but for some, there wasn't great sadness when the 1948 stadium was slated for replacement. Built for Denver's one-time Bears baseball team, and enlarged in the late 1950s to accommodate the Broncos, the old Mile High lacked amenities, parking and easy navigation. The stadium's main attribute was steel risers that allowed the region's super-fans to stomp up a storm and produce that special Denver noise known as "Rocky Mountain Thunder."

The use of metal for risers was one feature Fentress carried over into the new stadium, a project in association with architect HNTB Sports Entertainment. The studio also kept the horseshoe shape, but topped it with a sleek, steel swirl. The curvy crown makes INVESCO Field a surprising addition to the city's skyline. This highly visible landmark also complements the metal and glass wrapper on the upper section of the stadium, which rests on a solid brick base.

The presence of INVESCO Field at Mile High is inspired by two elements that reflect the Broncos' iconography: the horseshoe and the saddle. The stadium's proximity to Denver's downtown makes it a part of the city's urban core.

Parking is a given at a major sports facility, but Fentress pushed it back to locate the stadium in a park-like setting, offering space for fans to gather, celebrate or mourn (above).

Massive monitors ring the stadium's sleek crown, lighting the Denver skyline on game nights (right).

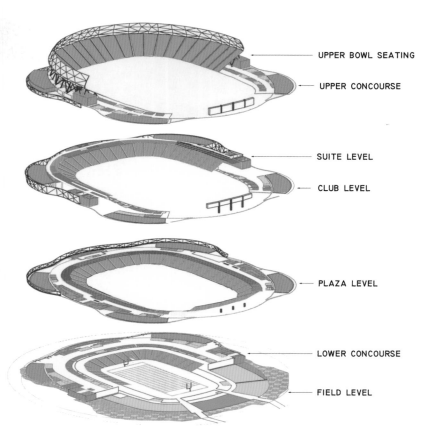

UPPER BOWL SEATING

UPPER CONCOURSE

SUITE LEVEL

CLUB LEVEL

PLAZA LEVEL

LOWER CONCOURSE

FIELD LEVEL

- ◼ SUITES
- ◼ SUPPORT / MECHANICAL EMPLOYEE FACILITIES
- ◼ CLUBS / NOVELTIES
- ◼ RESTROOMS
- ◼ VERTICAL CIRCULATION
- ◻ CONCESSIONS / FOOD SERVICE ADMINISTRATION
- ◼ SEATING

Different seating options – including suites and club seats – offer amenities to fans of all types in a stadium that is easy to enter, navigate and exit (above).

Under a Colorado blue sky, a sea of orange and blue signals that Broncos fans are ready for another spell of Rocky Mountain Thunder.

A TROPHY HOME

Over the years the vintage 1948 Bears baseball stadium was expanded in bits and pieces, and eventually became Mile High. First came the south stands, then the upper decks, and in 1977, the innovative east stands that could be moved in and out of position on a thin film of water to accommodate both football and baseball – all the better to share the space with the Broncos football club. A big push to snag a Major League Baseball team paid off in 1990, when the public voted to pay for the nostalgic Coors Field; a year later, Major League Baseball approved an expansion franchise for Denver. Not long after, the Denver Broncos began their own campaign for a new home, and the public again voted for financial support, leading to a gleaming and much more family-friendly INVESCO Field at Mile High in 2001.

The dark red brick carries a blue fleck, or iron spot, suggesting the team's colors of orange and blue. The bricks' texture catches the light, and signals an entrance that is easy to understand. The exterior of the building is unified by an aluminum structure that runs in a horizontal manner around the stadium. Some areas are open, allowing air and light into the ramps; areas that needed to be heated and cooled are glazed. The stadium cornice has the curvature of a saddle, carrying through the Broncos theme.

Fentress surrounded the stadium with a park setting and a natural environment, with plenty of space to gather. Yet this is a stadium with a difference: it's in the city, and master-planned to include amenities such as restaurants, shopping and year-round activities.

"We started out with the concept of a stadium in a park," says Curtis Fentress. "We created a green zone around the building, which gave us an opportunity to deal with the height change and elevations of parking lot areas. It gave us a setting for future urban integration."

The studio conducted numerous meetings with community groups and officials in the six county area (voters metro-wide approved the stadium district bonds). For a project of this magnitude, the studio drew upon principles that stress focus and patience, while paying close attention to the wishes of groups as diverse as the NFL, the team owner, city officials, fans and neighbors.

"We listened to the community during these meetings," says Fentress. "True football fans were happy to have a stadium dedicated to football. We made the seats wider and deeper. We put more bathrooms in the building, and more counters for food service. We built it out of steel. The whole building is steel plate, so the risers allow fans to make more noise than if it were a cold concrete structure."

The design also took a broader view, making a space that focused on football, but with an eye to a broad range of activities.

"At the time this building was designed, the NFL was thinking about the future, and the future was that football was something women enjoyed and was more of a family and social activity. With club levels, boxes and a Quarterback's Club, it appeals to the whole family, not just a bunch of guys drinking beer at a football game. This was the future – now."

On August 28, 2008, people jammed INVESCO – and stayed close to their televisions – to watch Democratic candidate Barack Obama accept his party's nomination for President of the United States.

WATERMARK LUXURY RESIDENCES

Location **Denver, Colorado**
Client **Watermark LLC**
Year **2008**

Curtis Fentress "The client wanted an urban oasis – the best of city life overlaid on charming, tree-lined streets. Our challenge here was to design a building that fit the urban context, while offering its residents a refuge filled with quiet beauty and unsurpassed amenities."

2

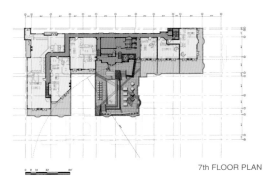

7th FLOOR PLAN

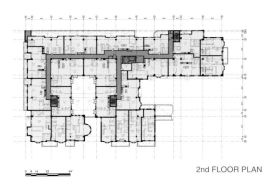

4th FLOOR PLAN

2nd FLOOR PLAN

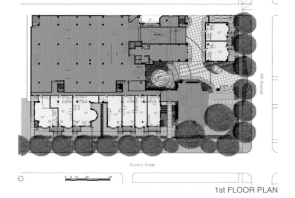

1st FLOOR PLAN

The Watermark Residences, tucked into Denver's historic Baker neighborhood, offer a different interpretation of "public architecture."

The 90 flats, brownstones and penthouses in this luxury residential development are by all definitions private. They come together at a Zen Courtyard, where illuminated, recycled glass boulders and subtle bamboo and moss lend contemplative qualities to a thriving urban neighborhood.

The issue of historic context prompted public participation, which in turn helped shape Fentress' design.

Zoning on the site allowed a high-rise to be built. But those living in nearby historic homes – an area with the largest concentration of Queen Anne residences in Denver – were concerned about the impact of a tower on the character of their neighborhood. The Watermark property also included a signature historic building, the Chittenden House, a mansion built in 1901 by a prominent Denver family. Over the years, it had been adapted for numerous uses, from a restaurant to a home for wayward boys.

Fentress' design for Watermark was not mimicry, not a Queen Anne theme park. Rows of two-story brownstones with contemporary lines anchor the seven-story building at a scale in balance with nearby homes. The brownstones are clad in brick, with white wooden porches and columns; these gestures, and numerous bay windows, exist in harmony with the neighborhood's prevalent architectural detailing.

Above the brownstone level, the building is stepped back, diminishing the overall mass. This effect is enhanced by walls colored a rich burnt umber that harmonizes with the brick and a pale cream that picks up on detailing. The top level, a floor devoted to penthouses and a Sky Garden with Denver's first infinity-edge pool, is stepped back even farther. This shields the majority of the building mass from eyes on the street, creating a retreat in the sky with stunning views of both Denver and the Rocky Mountains.

Building around the mansion meant "taking a bite out of the site." The resulting backward "F" shape proved a challenge, but one with an unforeseen bonus: mostly unduplicated floor plans that open up the building to lots of natural light and incredible views.

Interiors reflect the same attention to detail exhibited in the building's massing and volume. Cushioned ash plank floors deaden sound, and each home is wired for state-of-the-art audio and video systems. Kitchens are appointed in high-end appliances, with timeless and durable finishes. In response to Colorado's remarkable weather and views, most homes have spacious terraces, and large-scale windows and French doors are plentiful.

Inside and out, the focus is on residents' quality of life, immersed in a place that links vibrant urban living with the charm of historic surroundings, a secure place where old meets new, where water meets sky.

Two-story penthouses offer the luxury of separating private and public living areas, with entry corridors conceived as galleries for the display of art and artifacts. Most homes in Watermark feature solid ash plank hardwood floors installed over mats that help deaden noise, with lavish appointments in more personal spaces.

French doors and plentiful windows allow light to stream into the homes of Watermark, many of which open onto balconies and terraces that beckon the outdoors inside. High-end finishes, cabinets and appliances are standard throughout the flats, brownstones and penthouses.

Open floor plans offer the opportunity for ingenious solutions that divide areas psychologically, though favored art objects are never closed from view.

In this residence, a bedroom becomes a soothing private sanctuary from the buzz of daily life. Three "drops" of water – complete with puddles – offer an unexpected welcome to this penthouse. Mirrors fool the eye, directing it to mountain views beyond.

The roof-top Sky Garden doubles as a retreat for contemplation or a perfect party place, shielding residents and guests from activity below (following spread).

REBIRTH OF A NEIGHBORHOOD

What is now known as the Baker neighborhood south of downtown Denver boomed in the 1880s, resulting in the largest concentration of Queen Anne homes in the city. As a new millennium began, the area saw a wave of interest, with renovations and development pulling in a new generation of homeowners.

More than a century ago, the city's flush economy produced homes, schools and churches in Baker that often reflected the complexity of Victorian architecture, with its millwork and "gingerbread." But after the Silver Crash of 1893, design and decorative elements became much less elaborate — and expensive. That's true of one of the grandest mansions in Baker, the Chittenden House, built by financier Harry Chittenden in 1901 and designed by architects Albert J. Norton and Willis A. Marean. Though the Chittenden House displays the period's requisite dentils and pilasters with ornate capitals, it is a streamlined version of what might have been.

The construction of the Watermark Luxury Residences prompted renovation of the Chittendon House. With years of damage reversed, the Chittenden now houses offices, becoming an anchor for both its Victorian neighbors and an upscale contemporary development.

ARRAYA TOWER

Location **Kuwait City, Kuwait**
Client **Salhia Real Estate Company**
Year **2009**

Curtis Fentress "Tall buildings are city landmarks. The tallest buildings are the world's icons. City officials and private investors try to put themselves or their cities on the map by building one taller than someone else's. Architecture in the Middle East has become a spectator sport."

3

For a studio that uses context to create an identity for its buildings, designing a tower for the Arraya Centre in Kuwait City provided an unusual challenge. That's because the context was… more towers – tall, gleaming structures in a "bigger is better" race that has turned the Middle East into an architect's paradise.

The developer had set aside a specific site for Fentress: a corner of a popular, upscale complex that includes retail, office space and a hotel, all situated in the heart of Kuwait City's financial and business district. It was the studio's charge to shape a distinctive 60-story building, while amplifying a tall and slender profile.

The urban context certainly was there, but Fentress had no vernacular elements from which to draw.

"It is all new and modern, and it's a much more international style," says Curtis Fentress. "There is nothing historical around this building, not even a mosque, to which we could relate."

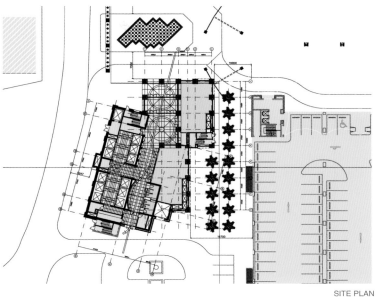

SITE PLAN

The Arraya Tower is integrated into Kuwait's busy Arraya Centre through careful siting (left) and architectural elements that recall other buildings in the complex. As the tallest building in Kuwait, Arraya offers superb views of the city and the Persian Gulf.

The diagonal braces (facing page) serve multiple purposes on the tower, which marries two design schemes into a slender whole (elevations below).

Ranking Number 4 on the list of tallest buildings completed in 2009 by the Council on Tall Buildings and Urban Habitat, Arraya Tower's slim profile and well-defined articulation give it a place of honor on the skyline.

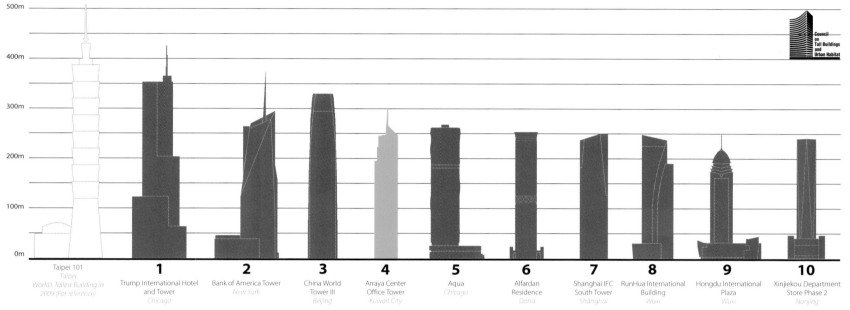

Taipei 101 *Taipei* *World's Tallest Building in 2009 (For reference)*	**1** Trump International Hotel and Tower *Chicago*	**2** Bank of America Tower *New York*	**3** China World Tower III *Beijing*	**4** Arraya Center Office Tower *Kuwait City*	**5** Aqua *Chicago*	**6** Alfardan Residence *Doha*	**7** Shanghai IFC South Tower *Shanghai*	**8** RunHua International Building *Wuxi*	**9** Hongdu International Plaza *Wuxi* **10** Xinjiekou Department Store Phase 2 *Nanjing*

© 2009 Council on Tall Buildings and Urban Habitat

Still, Fentress determined a way for the Arraya Tower to make peace with, yet stand out from, its neighbors: using complementary design schemes and materials woven together as a nod to the surrounding architecture. The design of the building reads as a soaring glass tower, with a façade set off by dynamic diagonal steel braces that fulfill both structural and aesthetic needs; they resist lateral wind loads while adding rhythm and definition to the building. The glass structure is topped by a communications mast at the peak of its sloped, diamond-shaped crown. But some sections are clad in limestone, with punched windows that recall similar elements of other buildings in the complex. At night, colored LED lights appear to zigzag up and down the glass tower, adding drama to the skyline.

"This distinction in materials worked together to make the building feel taller and slimmer," Fentress says.

The Council on Tall Buildings and Urban Habitat ranked the Arraya Tower as the fourth tallest building completed in 2009, putting it in the company of structures such as the Trump International Hotel and Tower in Chicago, the Bank of America Tower in New York, and the China World Trade Center III in Beijing.

Tall buildings – skyscrapers – are especially dependent on a healthy economy. They are expensive to build, require additional security elements, and demand ingenuity in incorporating sustainable elements.

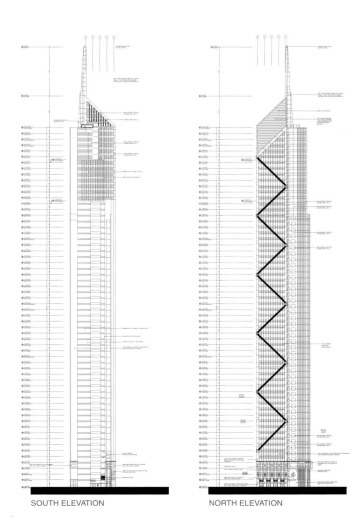

SOUTH ELEVATION   NORTH ELEVATION

The sustainable use of marble and high-performance glass sparks the luxurious entry to the tower, which offers tenants modern amenities and flexibility in configuring office spaces.

In the case of the Arraya Tower, the glass used is high-performance, with a low-U value and a high-shading co-efficient to contribute to an energy-efficient building. The design integrates state-of-the-art communications technology with the latest in high-rise requirements. It offers flexibility: raised floors allow easy access to power and teledata cabling, while tenant space can be easily reconfigured. Built with a concrete core and frame, Arraya includes three distinct zones, with different floor plates to break down the mass of the building and boost a slender profile.

Practical matters aside, Arraya's slim appearance on the skyline, well-articulated exterior, and elegant interior usher it into the special place reserved for skyscrapers, and the public's heart.

"You're designing landmarks, and it has its own reward," says Fentress. "I'm sure the people who designed the St. Louis Arch, the Golden Gate Bridge, or the Empire State Building all experienced a certain level of elation. These projects, by design, are the hearts of their cities and beloved by people around the world. They define the word timeless."

THE RISING CITY

Since the 1990 Iraqi invasion, Kuwait has repaired billions of dollars of damage, putting blown-out oil production facilities back on line and backing construction projects that have changed the face of the country. The oil fires took eight months to extinguish, with another two years spent returning production to its level before the attacks began on August 2 that year and concluded the following February. Aerial bombs laid waste to more than the nation's major export commodity; agriculture and fishing were impaired, and buildings leveled. Reconstruction of structures destroyed during the occupation continues. Although economic diversification has not moved as quickly as some might wish, in 2009, the country's National Assembly approved an economic development plan to spend up to $140 billion over a five-year period to shift economic emphasis away from oil production, and increase private-sector investment in economic

1999 BROADWAY

Location **Denver, Colorado**
Client **Lawder Corporation**
Year **1985**

Curtis Fentress "It was amazing we were able to pull it all together. We had to close an alley while we worked with the church, the Vatican, the bank, the developers, city planning and zoning, and all the code requirements. We were able to do all that and build a building that has become the city's landmark."

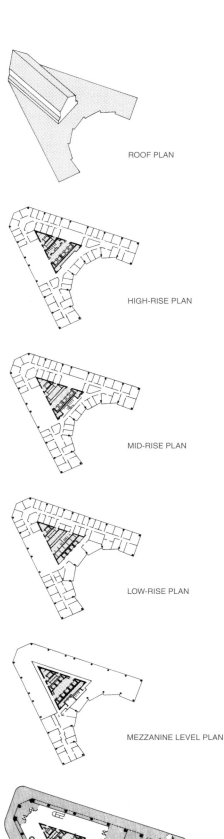

ROOF PLAN

HIGH-RISE PLAN

MID-RISE PLAN

LOW-RISE PLAN

MEZZANINE LEVEL PLAN

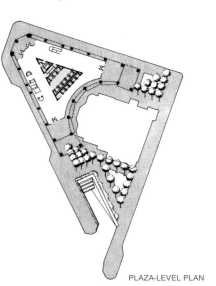

PLAZA-LEVEL PLAN

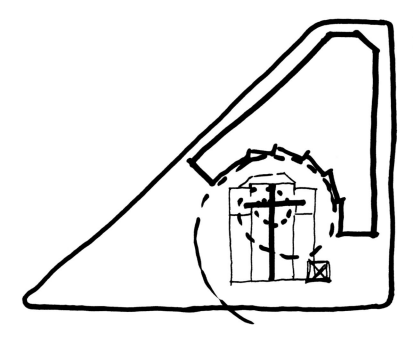

The arithmetic spiral that determined the placement of 1999 Broadway produced a building with a concave façade that embraces the Holy Ghost Catholic Church. Dash lines of green neon were later added to the building, creating the look of a finely tailored, top-stitched suit.

All architects must deal with restrictions. There are dimensions and topography, budget and program. And always, always, there are deadlines.

In the case of 1999 Broadway, though, Fentress had to deal with more than a tight, triangular piece of land on a prominent intersection that linked downtown Denver with historic close-in neighborhoods. There already was a building on part of the site, a designated landmark beloved by the community: the gemlike 1943 Holy Ghost Catholic Church designed in an American eclectic, Neo-Renaissance style by noted Denver architect Jacques Benedict.

But in booming early-1980s Denver, this was a rare piece of open land, and a developer wanted it for a new office tower. First, however, it was necessary to get approval from the Vatican. And the agreement required Fentress to restore Holy Ghost, while making sure the church could continue to serve its devoted parish day in and day out.

Fentress' studio was relatively new, and was looking for challenging design projects. 1999 Broadway provided just that, a new building and a renovation that required a solution both sensitive and innovative. The result was a respectful response to the church, while determining the new building's shape through the lines and setbacks created by the streets that define the site.

"We had a large and historic immoveable object, but the challenge of working around the church led us to the concept of an arithmetic spiral, which led us to the form," says Curtis Fentress.

The buff brick and terra cotta of the church exterior inspired the materials and color palettes of 1999 Broadway. The class A office building seems to embrace the historic church.

That idea involved designing a tower with two faces in two different materials palettes, while showcasing the historic landmark. Fentress used the cross plan of the church as the focal point. The façade facing Holy Ghost – a concave, multi-faceted reflective glass curtain wall – seems to sweep the church into its arms. This created three times the usual number of corner offices with mountain views – a developer's dream. On the tower's face into downtown, the answer was a soaring wall that features alternating bands of limestone and glass, presenting a clean edge to the city.

Lifting the tower off the ground with a series of 50-foot columns opened up the space for viewing the church, in the process creating a public plaza for contemplation and a break from the distraction of the city. The plaza also cemented the connection among the intersecting streets, the downtown business district, and other parts of the city.

A few years later, new owners contacted the studio, saying they wanted to run continuous green neon lighting on the outside edges of the building, boosting its presence on the skyline at night. It was an era in which exterior lighting was again gaining popularity in Denver. Instead, Fentress cautioned them to work from the inside, skipping floors but being able to use the existing electrical system and protect the lights from the city's sometimes harsh weather.

"This gives it a dash line that is distinctly different from buildings where the lights just trace the building's outline," Fentress says. "It's a much more artistic look."

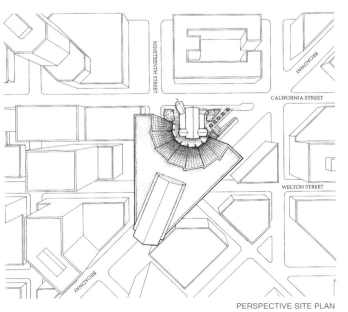

PERSPECTIVE SITE PLAN

1999 Broadway acts as a mirror for the church, while creating a plaza that has sparked activity in this downtown location.

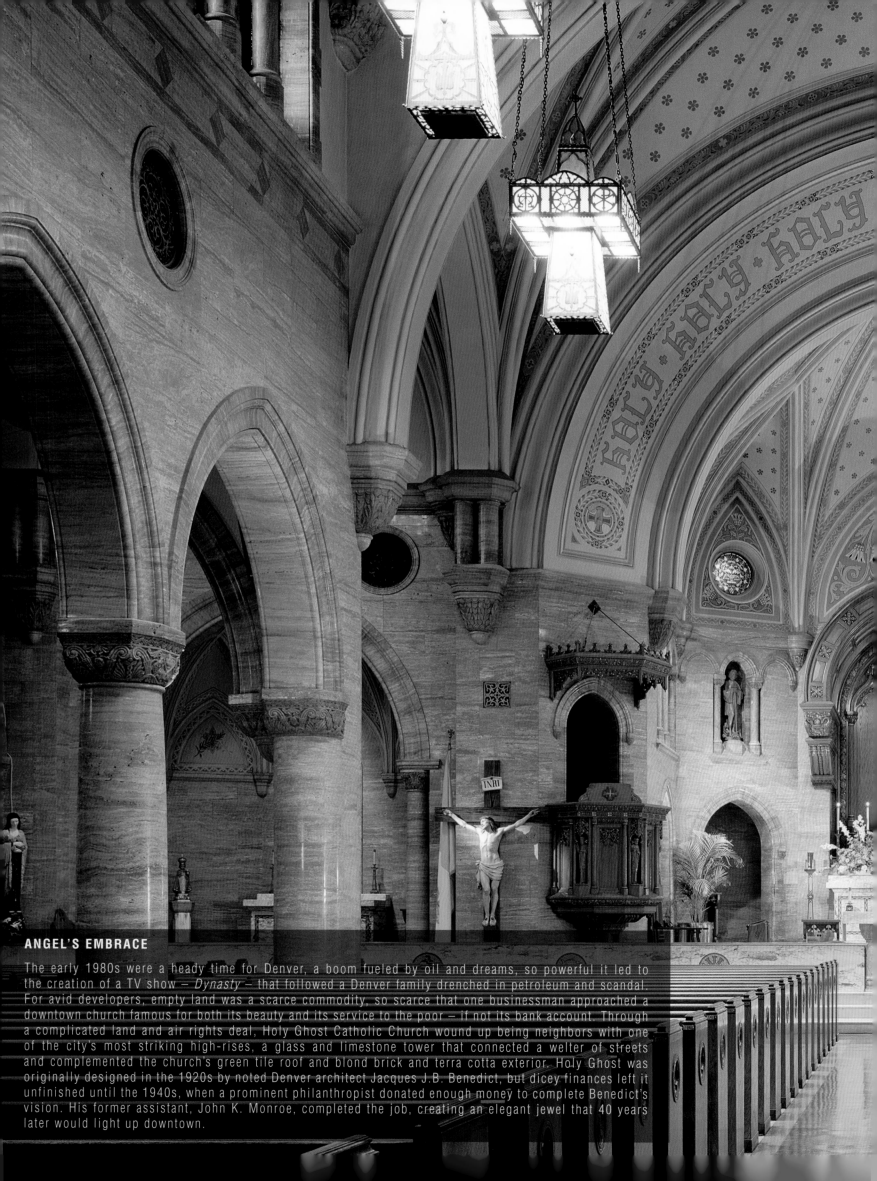

ANGEL'S EMBRACE

The early 1980s were a heady time for Denver, a boom fueled by oil and dreams, so powerful it led to the creation of a TV show – *Dynasty* – that followed a Denver family drenched in petroleum and scandal. For avid developers, empty land was a scarce commodity, so scarce that one businessman approached a downtown church famous for both its beauty and its service to the poor – if not its bank account. Through a complicated land and air rights deal, Holy Ghost Catholic Church wound up being neighbors with one of the city's most striking high-rises, a glass and limestone tower that connected a welter of streets and complemented the church's green tile roof and blond brick and terra cotta exterior. Holy Ghost was originally designed in the 1920s by noted Denver architect Jacques J.B. Benedict, but dicey finances left it unfinished until the 1940s, when a prominent philanthropist donated enough money to complete Benedict's vision. His former assistant, John K. Monroe, completed the job, creating an elegant jewel that 40 years later would light up downtown.

BELL TOWER

Location **Denver, Colorado**
Client **Paradise Land Company**
Year **Unknown**

5

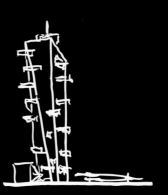

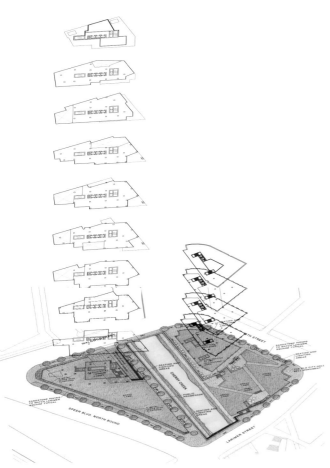

LANDSCAPE PLAN

The residential Bell Tower, with its glass skin and torqued profile, is accompanied by a smaller office and retail building in stone and brick. Both offer access to Cherry Creek and help link lower downtown and a university campus across a major thoroughfare. Its location on one of Denver's oldest streets is now a magnet of hot restaurants and retail.

The tiny, triangular site called Bell Park was hardly a household name. In fact, "park" was really a glorified term for an oddly shaped, somewhat scruffy parking lot that contained a large bronze bell, a reminder that Denver's first city hall had once stood on this location.

But then developer Buzz Geller commissioned a design for a tall, slim and transparent luxury tower that would be like nothing Denver or the region had ever seen before. Bell Park's anonymous status quickly changed, as Fentress' design for a statuesque clear and green glass residential tower became the talk of the town. Not only would each floor be a single home, but the project would include uncommonly generous balconies.

"There would be backyards in the sky," says Curtis Fentress. "No other building would have this type of connection to the outdoors and the incredible Colorado mountain views."

After months of discussion over height limitations imposed by the proposed location in the city's lower downtown historic district, the land for Bell Tower was removed from the district and the restrictions lifted. This choice piece of land offers access to the historically important Cherry Creek, while linking downtown and lower downtown to a major university campus across busy Speer Boulevard.

As part of the project, Fentress also designed an adjacent retail and office building that is significantly smaller. It displays two materials palettes, showing a more contemporary face toward Speer, and a more historic one toward lower downtown. Here, too, the Bell Tower project serves as a bridge, reflecting the stone of the central business district and the brick of LoDo's mercantile structures.

For such a small piece of land, Bell Park now wields amazing clout, with the promise of adding a glittering, one-of-a-kind presence to Denver's skyline.

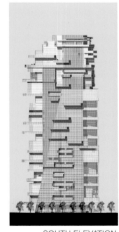

NORTH ELEVATION   EAST ELEVATION   SOUTH ELEVATION   WEST ELEVATION

Clear and green glass transform Bell Tower into a beacon on the skyline, while helping to create an edge for the city's downtown business district and Lower Downtown Historic District.

Location **Dubai, United Arab Emirates**
Client **The Private Office of H.H. Sheikh Saed Bin Zayed Al-Nahayyan**
Year **2012**

6

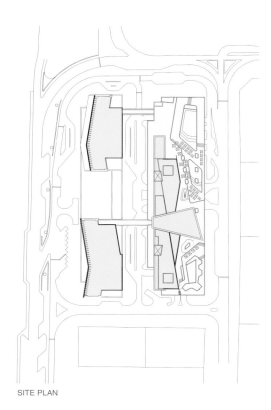

SITE PLAN

The sinuous Dubai Towers appear to dance on the skyline, but are firmly rooted in a broad podium comprising restaurants, parking, and other amenities.

A rendering of the Dubai cityscape shows the Dubai Towers adjacent to the world's tallest building, the Burj Khalifa. The Dubai Towers' hotel spa will feature an eye-catching green glass entry, a gem glowing on the skyline (following spread).

The culture of Dubai stretches back for millennia, as a port city, as a center of pearl diving, and as a key stop on the route that sent spices around the known world. Dubai was small, exotic and devoted to the art of the deal.

The Dubai of today began with the discovery of oil in 1966. This emirate might not be sitting on as much black gold as its neighbors, but the money Dubai did amass it invested in infrastructure, the base for a massive urban expansion designed to attract people looking for fun, business, architectural riches, and major-league shopping.

Dubai at heart will always be a port city, a place where the business of business is business. A building boom on steroids over the last 15 years has produced spectacular structures, each straining to be taller and bigger than the last. But if a recession means it may be a while before anyone tops the Burj Khalifa, the world's tallest building, other projects proceed. This includes a building right next door: Fentress' playful take on context and culture.

The Dubai Towers stand approximately 700 feet tall, a pair of shimmering skyscrapers whose glass and fretted glass curtain walls appear to bend and fold geometrically as they rise. The two shapes play off one another on the skyline, seeming to sway rhythmically atop a four-story podium that connects the towers. A veil-like folded sheet of glass overlaps the entire front façade, creating the sense of a patterned sunscreen and a distant architectural mirage. Instead, this is a real-time project with upscale amenities, including a spa that sparkles like a faceted gem at night, and a pool that offers indoor and outdoor access for swimming as the night grows cool.

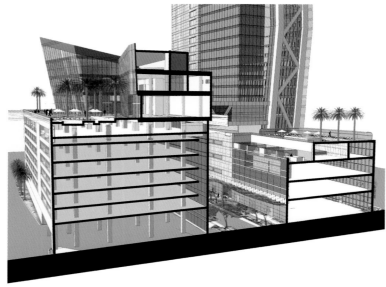

LOBBY SECTION

Over the course of design, the project picked up nicknames that aim at both locale and custom: "The Spice Girls", a nod to Dubai's one-time prominence as a player in the spice trade between India and the Arab countries, and the "Dancing Sisters", for the role of dance in Dubai's indigenous culture.

" 'Dancing Sisters' is something that our clients and I came up with together in a meeting," says Curtis Fentress. "First I said, 'brothers,' and our clients said, 'Why not sisters?' "

Whimsy aside, the studio needed to address practical matters in order to team the sculptural forms with the efficiency necessary for a tower. To create the appearance of two towers seemingly moving in cadence, an innovative structural system was devised to let floors extend beyond the core support: a framework of diagonal braces ties together sections of cantilevered floors. Each floor plate is shifted slightly in relationship to a stable vertical core that accommodates utilities.

The complex will house a five-star hotel and spa, luxury offices and residences, conference centers, retail, dining and entertainment areas. It will be marked by a green-glass crystal entry, a sparkling addition laid at the feet of the "Dancing Sisters".

Wallace Chan

Wallace Chan translates ancient Chinese philosophy into contemporary art in the form of jewelry and sculpture. Curtis Fentress interprets the ever-changing needs of contemporary urban communities into public space. Though they work in different mediums, each artist decodes cues from our daily lives and collective consciousnesses, transforming them into sensory and spiritual experiences of eternal beauty.

Through a personal bond that has stretched over five years and across the Eastern/Western divide, Wallace and Curtis, both in the avant-garde of their respective fields, have discovered their many similarities. The most obvious is their passion to pioneer innovative engineering solutions while incorporating unorthodox materials into their work, such as Wallace's mastery of titanium in his wearable art, and Curtis' bold use of fabric to cover the terminal of Denver International Airport.

Each of their designs – inspired by history, people and nature – aims to expand cultural horizons, and transcend time and territory. Light is the key that opens the doors to Curtis' architecture and Wallace's discovery of a gemstone's soul – the harnessed power of light awakens the spirit, soothes it, and creates an illuminated, joyful encounter for the individual who walks these spaces or views the sculptures.

While Curtis continues to hone his talents in the realm of public architecture, Wallace forges on in the experimental world of titanium jewelry sculpture, each artist constantly breaking through into new and unexplored territory. In order to elucidate on the main subject of this book, i.e., Curtis' work, it seems fitting to discuss the innovations of Wallace Chan in order to offer a deeper insight into the relationship between sculptural jewelry and architecture, and the interconnectedness of these two master builders.

The choice of Beijing's Capital Museum as the venue for Wallace Chan's retrospective exhibition – displayed in a seductive, darkened room with Chinese classical music in the background – firmly links

Wallace's groundbreaking work to the museum's vast collectio of early to late dynasty Buddha carvings, jewelry and works ca in metal. It was Lao Tzu's (5th century BCE) belief that, limited b nature, one must create within its confines. It is within these confine that Wallace finds unlimited possibilities. By combining nature precious and semi-precious stones (the ancient) with the new-ag metal titanium (the contemporary) he carves and casts an origina never-before-seen artistic language. Wallace believes that stone technical knowledge and talent are not enough to create art: the arti must approach his work with an honest heart, open to experience bot sensual and metaphysical, which can then serve as a conduit to tap int the mysterious and divine powers of creativity.

Wallace grew up in a traditional Chinese home in Fuzhou, the capita city of Fujian province, known for its long tradition of stone carver As a young boy, under the critical and watchful eye of his maste he honed his sculpting skills through trial and error. By adolescenc carving became Wallace's life passion.

Using the self-reliant method learned from his Chinese maste he traveled throughout Europe and taught himself the Western a of cameo and intaglio relief carving. He experimented with differer materials such as turquoise, tourmaline, crystals, and aquamarin onto which he carved Greek and Roman mythological figure By combining Chinese techniques and skill with the Europea tradition, he was able to break down the barrier between Eastern an Western thinking and their different approaches to carving.

The stage was set for his first breakthrough. Wallace began combinin faceting – a method of geometric cutting that brings out the life an fire in a stone – with figurative intaglio carving. The result of h experimentations ended with his inventing the "Wallace Cut ," whic won the prestigious Hong Kong Jewelry Design Grand Award in 1987 The innovative "Wallace Cut" was essentially a form of sculpture tha combined abstract and figurative techniques, utilizing the crystal

herent reflective properties. In his sculpture *Horae*, for example, Wallace carved a relief image into a large smoky quartz crystal, and then faceted the peripheries around it so that the image reflected onto three planes. One goddess, her image reflected three times, represents each of the three Greek goddesses who controlled the seasons.

Within a frozen world of light, they seem to peer at the viewer with Mona Lisa eyes from whichever angle the work is viewed. Wallace's technique fragmented perspective through reflection – like mirrors in a funhouse – leaving the viewer to question, in Taoist fashion, the notions of reality and illusion. The original concept of the three *Horae* goddesses actually being the reflection of one can be read as Wallace's belief that there is one world and one humanity, with multiple perspectives and religions.

Elevated to the top of various trades at a precocious age (he also completed an engineering course), there seemed no end to Wallace's creative and material successes – until he suffered a spiritual crisis. He embraced Buddhism, meditated frequently in the mountains, and spent much of the 1990s employing his talent to create large-scale sculptures for temples and monasteries across Asia. Through meditation the concept of titanium – his next revolutionary breakthrough – kept coming to him as a vision.

Titanium allowed Wallace's imagination to be the limit, not weight or material. Possessing the highest strength-to-weight ratio of any metal – strong as steel and almost 50 percent lighter – we see here the duality of spirituality (lightness) combined with materialism (weight) in our industrializing world – all qualities contained within Wallace the man, and his work.

Nature, travel, modern art and human relations became sources of Wallace's inspiration. In keeping with his natural and lifelong inclination for innovation, Wallace combined the fruits of his titanium experiments and new life experiences with his earlier revolutionary

carving techniques. By synthesizing his two groundbreaking innovations, Wallace was able to push the boundaries of sculpture and jewelry to a level not seen since the golden years of the Art Deco era. From his spiritual cocoon of crisis Wallace emerged transformed as a master jeweler, and in turn has metamorphosed how the world views and appreciates jewelry as art.

The metamorphosis is not just a metaphor: as in his brooch entitled *I Am Still Dancing*, Wallace uses real butterfly wings in his creations, vacuum-sealed in crystal on which he carves designs that reflect the dialogue between light and gems, sun and nature.

Like traditional Chinese ink painters who evoked detail with seemingly simple brush strokes, Wallace, with his specially minted tools, creates titanium animals, flowers and insects down to their minutest details – like the fine hairs on a cicada's leg found in his sculptural brooch entitled *Zen* or in the bubbles emanating from a goldfish's mouth, so that the glass showcase seems transformed into an aquarium of marine life.

As well as true-to-life renderings of nature through titanium and stone, Wallace also creates contemporary abstract expressions with explosive strokes of light and color, exemplified in his work entitled *The Birth of Light*. In each of his works, Wallace employs innovations of engineering such as setting stones with finely carved precious stone claws instead of traditional metal prongs, or invisibly setting diamonds into the carvings themselves so they appear suspended like stars in the sky.

Another combination of seemingly disparate concepts and never-before-used materials is Wallace's use of ancient objects. In *Return of the King* he incorporates a Qin dynasty white nephrite carving into a futuristic blue titanium bangle; a Qianlong period snuff bottle into the center of *His Majesty's Treasure*; and a 19th-century enameled Egyptian revival Pharaoh's head suspended in a necklace of reptiles in *Pharaoh*. By preserving the old, Wallace creates the new, thereby shedding deeper light and understanding on how our collective pasts and civilizations shape our present times.

Wallace expresses his beloved Buddhist ideas through a unique medium of precious stones and titanium. Like his name, which combines both Chinese and English, Wallace Chan's work should be understood within the universal concept of the Yin and Yang. He unites ancient Greek deities with the Buddha, old and new, light and dark, male and female. With an artistic gift for carving and design, a scientist's use of controlled experiments, and an engineer's technical savvy, Wallace has created a new art form out of stones and metal by harnessing the laws of nature.

The wall that has separated jewelry from art, spirituality from materialism, has been dismantled, and endless possibilities of combinations are now available for future generations to build upon. Wallace Chan not only had the courage to confront the spiritual crisis that almost debilitated him – having emerged stronger and illuminated through self-actualization – he also has the courage to selflessly share the wealth of knowledge he gained on the way for any dreamer to tap into.

This self-knowledge and mastery hinges on what is truthful, timeless and full of light, a state of mind that has also propelled Curtis Fentress' designs to a new level. Within the literal and figurative spaces of these two artists, the individual can experience the eternity of a universal moment that is at once natural and man-made.

Andrew Cohen
Contributing Editor for *Art Asia Pacific Magazine*
Filmmaker

SPIRITUAL AND PSYCHOLOGICAL MYSTERY

Wallace Chan creates unique works using a wide range of materials — from rock crystal to titanium — confronting the challenge each one presents. For the inscrutable sculptural piece *Struggling for a Way Out*, Chan turned to obsidian, a glass-like rock formed when lava is cooled by water, to carve a carefully draped cloak of darkness from which a man is breaking free. The figural portion of the piece is cast in silver, displaying strong musculature and veining in the partially visible limbs.

TITANIUM JEWELRY: THE LIGHTNESS OF BEING

It took years for Wallace Chan to master the technique of revealing color in this naturally gray metal. But he conquered the challenge because titanium's light weight allows him to take advantage of the fact that the metal is both hard and light, about one-fifth the weight of gold. Thus his sculptural jewelry can be larger and more complex, yet still wearable.

CUTTING JADE: HOMAGE TO A STONE

The Chinese consider jade the pinnacle of gems, and thus Wallace Chan approaches it with respect. However, he also aims for a contemporary look, and to that end has created a technique that refines and brightens the stone to amplify the effect of light on the surface.

SETTING GEMS: INNOVATIVE CRAFTSMANSHIP

Traditional jewelry uses metal for the prongs and settings for gemstones. Wallace Chan has moved beyond that to define a way to use diamonds and other stones as the actual settings, not just the prized centerpiece. His inventions include the diamond claw setting and the inner mortise and tenon setting method, in which the gem or pearl in question is cut in such a way that it forms an invisible joint and a perfect fit.

COMMUNITY

SEMPER FIDELIS MEMORIAL PARK AND CHAPEL
THE CHAPEL AT CHERRY HILLS COMMUNITY CHURCH
MILE HI CHURCH

COMMUNITY

Communities change as people change. From family to school to city to workplace to world, we look for our mark on the stage in the theater called life.

Public architecture is, by nature, all about community. How people relate to their government, get an education, cheer on a team, travel, and absorb art or history. The community that strikes the deepest chord may be that of religion, where people gather to mark births and deaths, weddings and funerals, and the simple act of coming together with others to find solace, reflection, and peace.

Designing a place of worship is a delicate balance, since the building must achieve two things at the same time. A religious building should evoke a sense of awe, an acknowledgement of a spiritual presence and purpose in coming together. Yet the same building cannot overwhelm or look down on those who enter. All become equal, and as with effective public architecture, all must feel welcome.

Fentress understands the need to find a quiet monumentality in a house of worship, since it is a place for fellowship as well as

In the case of the Semper Fidelis Memorial Chapel, a gem on the park surrounding the National Museum of the Marine Corps, the studio's goal was to recall the field chapels hurriedly put up on battlefields so that soldiers could find tranquility in the midst of chaos. It is a small, simple place. Stone, wood and glass merge to offer a transparency that allows the surrounding green space to become one with the building. For weddings and memorials, Semper Fi holds the promise of an unpretentious setting elevated by honest materials.

The ministers of Mile Hi Church wanted to take another path, to continue the campus' emphasis on distinct, even provocative, architecture. Mile Hi serves a growing congregation drawn by inclusive teachings that rely on music for much of their power. Here, Fentress found the solution in a domed church, but not made of the traditional stone; instead, this big white bubble is an inflated and reinforced fabric roof membrane that announces its location blocks away. This innovative structure is in sync with the original church, also domed but with an unusual spider-shaped support system. The new worship space offered a financially savvy way to build, adding sustainable practices to reduce energy costs – but not impact.

The leaders of Cherry Hills Community Church fill their 5,000-seat main sanctuary with ease, a testimony to the congregation's sense of life-long community. There also, though, was a need to refine the campus with a smaller, more intimate and finely detailed chapel, in this instance, a stone structure that mixes traditional European charm with contemporary gestures. Fentress relied on the use of fine wood for furnishings, a stage and a soaring trussed ceiling that adds loft to the sanctuary. Abstracted forms brighten abundant stained-glass windows, letting light wash through the chapel, bringing peace and hope.

Refuge, support and serenity mark these communities, where different design approaches all lead to a higher goal.

SEMPER FIDELIS MEMORIAL PARK AND CHAPEL

Location **Quantico, Virginia**
Client **Marine Corps Heritage Foundation**
Year **2009**

1

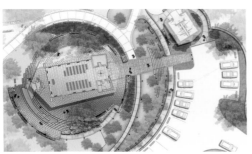

SITE PLAN

Parkland connects the National Museum of the Marine Corps and the Semper Fidelis Memorial Chapel, where rows of benches allude to the ammo-box pews found in field chapels.

A deep overhang mediates light allowed in by the expanse of glass that links the chapel to the surrounding woods (following spread).

At the dedication of the Semper Fidelis Memorial Chapel, the head of the Marine Corps Heritage Foundation spoke from the heart, as a man steeped in the history of the Corps.

"What we have created here is truly a national treasure," Lieutenant General Ron Christmas told the audience.

Down the hill from the chapel sits the National Museum of the Marine Corps, where a soaring glass skylight, shot through with a steel mast, protects a repository for the long history of the Corps.

But the museum is set in a far different environment, a park that is the essence of serenity. Named after the Corps' motto – *always faithful* – Semper Fidelis Memorial Park also shelters a rare jewel, a compact, contemplative chapel surrounded by stands of trees. The small but powerful Semper Fidelis Memorial Chapel brings focus to the park and offers a commanding hilltop view of the museum below.

The museum and chapel are both Fentress designs, and offer pure point/counterpoint, in impact and scale.

"The chapel is designed to be simple and humble," says Curtis Fentress. "Like a field chapel, it offers a private space for an introspective moment."

The 77-seat chapel hosts weddings and memorials, while remaining connected to the outdoors. It is all wood, stone and glass, a nearly transparent space built of natural fieldstone, with heavy timber columns and trusses. A steeply sloped slate roof completes the austere profile, which reaches skyward, as if chasing hope. It is the elegant embodiment of the field chapels pitched on battlefields and lonely bases around the world. The seats are wooden rectangles, recalling ammo-box pews; the sharply defined roof suggests a tarp hung up in the woods.

"This place speaks a soldier's language, and relates to their experiences," says Fentress.

THE CHAPEL AT CHERRY HILLS COMMUNITY CHURCH

Location **Highlands Ranch, Colorado**
Client **Cherry Hills Community Church**
Year **2006**

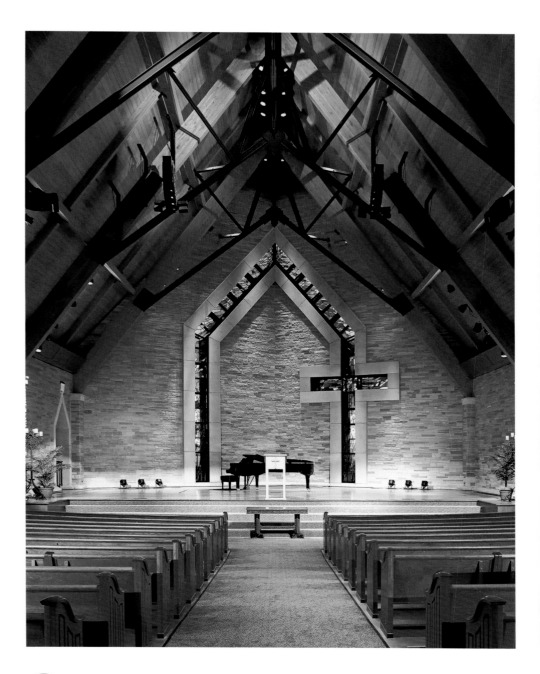

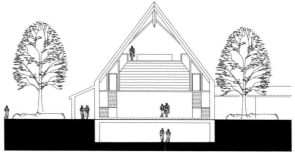

The sanctuary of the Chapel at Cherry Hills Community Church appears to expand because of the loft created by the pitched ceiling fortified by trusses and beams.

Interior details such as a spiral staircase add intimacy and a human scale to the stone chapel, in which clean, contemporary lines reinterpret a traditional church profile (following spread).

C herry Hills Community Church is a mega-force in the mega-community of Highlands Ranch, south of Denver. With seating for almost 5,000 people at each service, the church offers programs for members from the time they can walk until they settle into their senior years.

But church officials wanted to add something different to this formidable campus, something more intimate for special events such as weddings, funerals and memorials: a chapel focused on a sense of private communion with friends and family.

Officials called Fentress to design the chapel, along with cloister, garden-like settings, and the support facilities needed for special events and small receptions. The site offers a panoramic view of the Rocky Mountains, as well as the surrounding community.

For this commission, Fentress provided a traditional design rendered in clean, contemporary lines, with enduring materials such as sandstone and limestone walls, a natural slate roof, and an interior enlivened by the generous use of rich, gleaming cherry wood.

"We wanted to make the chapel as humanistic as possible, a small space that has warmth and quiet elegance," says Curtis Fentress.

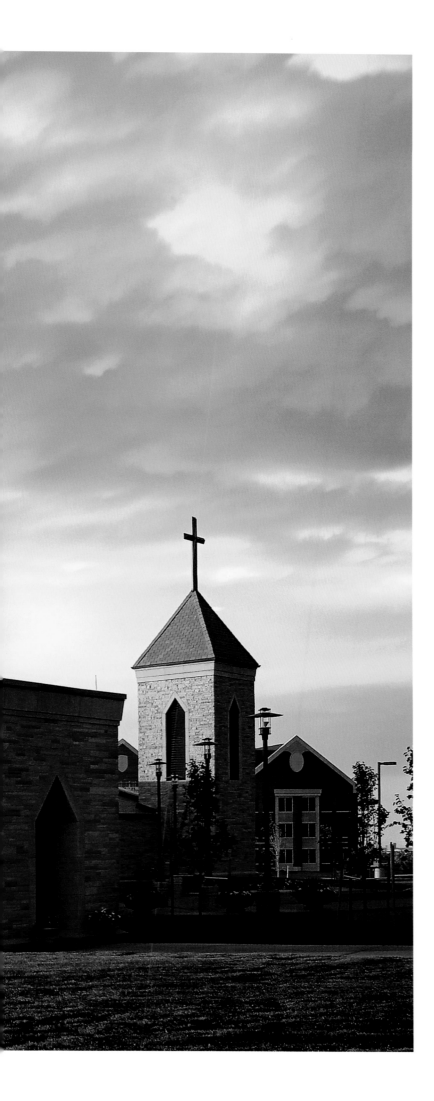

To achieve that effect, Fentress studied numerous sacred buildings, including the historic Evans Chapel at the University of Denver, nestled in a garden setting on campus. The Chapel at Cherry Hills Community Church reflects the same idea of privacy, offering a place for reflection amidst the beauty of natural materials.

The 350-seat chapel is dignified by interior stone walls and a soaring ceiling finished in cherry and supported by a series of wooden beams and steel scissor trusses. Rising over the nave and a spacious balcony at the rear of the sanctuary the ceiling adds loft to the building without distracting from visitors' focus on a cherry stage for religious services and performances. With a lift that can move a grand piano up and down as needed, the stage also draws attention to a large, asymmetrical stained glass window reflecting Christian iconography while tracing the outline of the chapel. Numerous other stained glass windows displaying abstracted floral forms line the chapel's hallways and arcades. All were fabricated by Rohlf's Stained and Leaded Glass of Mount Vernon, New York.

For this thriving Christian community, Fentress has interpreted spirituality in stone, and turned the intangible into the timeless.

MILE HI CHURCH

Location **Lakewood, Colorado**
Client **Mile Hi Church of Religious Science**
Year **2008**

3

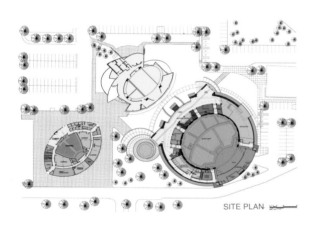

SITE PLAN

The new Mile Hi Church sanctuary is linked to the congregation's former place of worship through the shape and symbolism of a dome, unifying the campus.

The universal appeal of a dome lies in its suggestion of unity, making it suitable for building types as varied as a courthouse, a sports stadium and a church. In the last instance, though, a dome can recall the celestial, and when it supports an all-seeing eye, it evokes an aura of life's mystery.

For Mile Hi Church, an inclusive congregation in a suburb west of Denver, Fentress used innovative dome technology for the new sanctuary for a practical reason: topping its new 1,500-seat worship center with an inflated dome cut the cost substantially compared to using steel for a traditional roof form.

The church wanted the new space to express the same meditative quality as the old sanctuary. The project resulted in the largest dome building in the metro area, with a diameter of 232 feet and a height of 60 feet. Working from the interior, the fabric roof membrane was inflated, insulated and reinforced with steel rebar and a concrete coating to form the dome. It appears to hover over the building, which is embraced by a brick structure that provides space for an entry, prefunction, and circulation.

"We saw this construction technique as a way to make this work for the church's budget," says Fentress. "Necessity is the mother of invention. DIA's fabric roof follows the same principle. We wanted a free span in this large space, using materials we could afford, while not forgetting that a sacred space requires a certain kind of beauty."

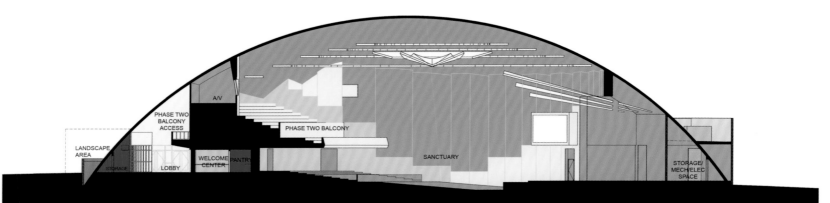

LANDSCAPE
AREA

PHASE TWO
BALCONY
ACCESS

A/V

PHASE TWO BALCONY

STORAGE

LOBBY

WELCOME
CENTER

PANTRY

SANCTUARY

STORAGE/
MECH/ELEC
SPACE

SECTION

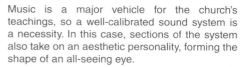

Music is a major vehicle for the church's teachings, so a well-calibrated sound system is a necessity. In this case, sections of the system also take on an aesthetic personality, forming the shape of an all-seeing eye.

The domed sanctuary, designed to expand via a 600-seat balcony, is the most recent addition to Mile Hi's campus of eye-catching buildings, including the 1973 "spider building," sporting its own dome and designed by Thomas William Hite, and the sleek 1998 administration building designed by Brendle APV.

The sanctuary's event-sized stage, raked theater seating, and state-of-the-art audio/visual and lighting equipment create a cutting-edge yet energy-efficient venue for services and performances. Yet the most striking interior element is an array of speakers suspended from the ceiling, forming the shape of that all-seeing eye. Emitting a joyful sound, this design again relies on a forward-thinking solution mixing the artful and the functional.

dancers and
constructed space
move harmoniously together

The intricate connection between movement and architecture has much to do with the fact that both disciplines share a common concern: that is, the manipulation of space through the medium of moving bodies and the built environment. DJ Spooky has said that dance offers a method of "interpreting the space around you." Just as the body bends and curves within perpetually morphing surroundings and strives to engage with the space around it by testing its own limits and abilities, the materials and structures of buildings seek to evoke the very character of space.

Choreographer Carol Brown has also spoken of the commonalities between dance and architecture, and asserts that for both, "the first experienced space is the space of the body." Curtis Fentress' aesthetic is likewise one that celebrates the body in motion – whether that be the body of the building or the bodies of the people moving through it.

Fentress' "Dancing Sisters," a 1.5-million-square-foot complex in Dubai, is an intricate structure that pivots on the centrality of motion. Two lithe, elegant towers of glass and metal shimmer sinuously and give the appearance of undulating, sensual forms. The effect, steeped as it is in slopes and angles, is one of light being refracted off multiple surfaces. Folded sheets of glass bend and crease, like a body, offering a glorious oasis and visual feast in the midst of the desert. It is an

approach that is expressive, elegant and innovative. Rather than overpowering the environment with an artificially manufactured building that refutes environmental context, Fentress seeks to harmonize organic, symmetrical forms with their surroundings and cultural context.

This is an aesthetic that also denies the static nature of space; rather, space is something that is produced not just by the building that contains it, but also by movement. As one of Fentress' principles makes clear, "As people move through a building, they help shape it. It's a natural flow." Additionally, Fentress has always stressed that a public building must tell the story of a community and the people who occupy it; while it may also have its own tale to tell, it must not overpower the people it serves.

Similarly, architect Frances Bronet, who developed two dance pieces with New York-based choreographer Ellen Sinopoli, has examined the intellectual and physical relationship between dance and architecture. Like Fentress' work, these are pieces that explore the question of whether or not space can be transformed by the way people move through it. Bronet draws a distinction between the kind of space manufactured by athletes or dancers – who are constantly working in the context of space in movement, or "space

the architecture. It's as if you had the theme of a piece of music in the middle, and on each side, architecturally, you had the beginning and the end of the music. But you let this piece in the middle be the crescendo."

The architectural vocabulary of the building was deeply informed by one of the primary activities that takes place at the civic auditorium – music. The composition of the building during the design process was akin to the creation of a score. The various components of the building were conceptualized with regard to proportion and interconnection, so the three structures constituting the building are harmoniously linked together by a common rhythm that results in a visually symphonic effect.

Goethe's description of architecture as "frozen music" was perhaps more aligned with his interpretation of the dominant Baroque style of his time, whose fluid, graceful curves appeared to be the very representation of all things protean and elusive. Daniel Libeskind purportedly only began to explore architecture after a long love affair with the accordion and several successful performances with audiences, which prompted him to consider the emotive (and potentially cathartic) link between music and architecture as objects of contemplation.

Further, recent studies of music and architecture have paid more scrutiny to structure, which is the very cornerstone of both disciplines. Perhaps this is something that Zaha Hadid also considered when conceptualizing the J.S. Bach Chamber Music Hall in Manchester, England, which was especially designed for solo chamber music performances. A rippling steel structure encased by a transparent acrylic membrane, it offers the appearance of ribbons enclosing the performance area. Visually, it's a mathematically precise structure that suggests a three-dimensional representation of Bach's eloquent, complex, layered fugues. Hadid herself has noted, "The design enhances the multiplicity of Bach's work through a coherent integration of formal and structural logic," with layered spaces that effectively "cocoon the performers and audience within an intimate fluid space." The very structure of the building, while striving to achieve unison with the work being performed within it, is capable of coloring and shaping an audience's experience. This sensitivity to the visual expression of a building as a function of its use, as well as a visceral response to other art forms, can also be related to the rhythmic, sloping beauty of Fentress' "Dancing Sisters."

In exploring the relationship between dance, architecture and music, it's evident that when differing art forms shift and merge, they are capable of creating rich, interdisciplinary dialogues and generating work that is unexpected and new.

defined by how the players create openings" – and many of the spaces that people typically inhabit, which are predictable and defined by known boundaries. In the movement piece *Beating a Path*, Bronet and Sinopoli challenge their dancers to use all available surfaces of the building. A major concept that the work accentuates is the dissolution of boundaries between dance and architecture. In the piece, both dancers and constructed space move harmoniously together. By virtue of a rolling platform, as dancers run in one direction, the floor slides in the opposite direction – literalizing the metaphor of being able to manipulate built environments by virtue of the bodies that move through them.

This sort of experimentation with the mobility of both the human body and constructed space, as well as the manipulation of the built environment so that both appear to act in the same manner as human bodies, can also be found in the work of dance luminary Merce Cunningham. Cunningham's final work, *Nearly Ninety* (2009), was created in collaboration with Barcelona-based architect Benedetta Tagliaube, who designed the multi-tier set used by the dancers. In fact, comprehending the work of Merce Cunningham is akin to contemplating a Fentress building; both are executed with an enormous amount of technical expertise and artistic virtuosity. Because the performance involves a relationship with space in which dancers occupy multiple areas of focus, interpreting the piece is similar to the manner in which you might experience a Fentress building. Both, of necessity, must be fluid and adaptable to the needs of their inhabitants.

Like dance and architecture, music also evokes a sculptural component. The sonic environment is one that is integral to Fentress designs, such as the Pasadena Convention Center, which involved adding a new structure to a historic setting. Curtis Fentress has said, "We wanted the two new convention center buildings to be bookends to the Pasadena Civic Auditorium, to pick up the rhythm and carry it into

with layered spaces that effectively "cocoon the performers and audience within an intimate fluid space."

6

CIVIC + GOVERNMENT

CLARK COUNTY GOVERNMENT CENTER
JEFFERSON COUNTY GOVERNMENT CENTER
JEFFERSON COUNTY HUMAN SERVICES BUILDING
OAKLAND ADMINISTRATION BUILDINGS
SACRAMENTO CITY HALL
NATURAL RESOURCES BUILDING
SAN JOAQUIN COUNTY ADMINISTRATION BUILDING
CALIFORNIA DEPARTMENT OF EDUCATION HEADQUARTERS

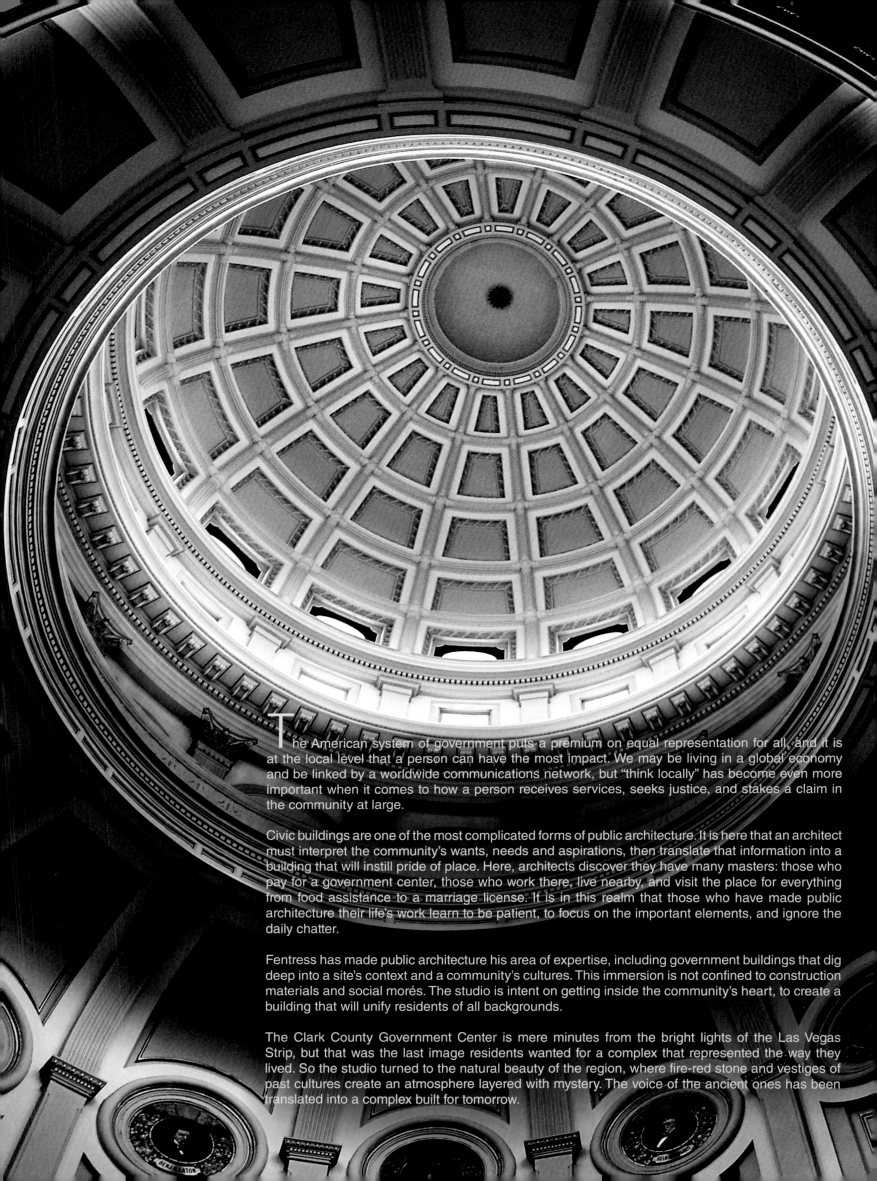

The American system of government puts a premium on equal representation for all, and it is at the local level that a person can have the most impact. We may be living in a global economy and be linked by a worldwide communications network, but "think locally" has become even more important when it comes to how a person receives services, seeks justice, and stakes a claim in the community at large.

Civic buildings are one of the most complicated forms of public architecture. It is here that an architect must interpret the community's wants, needs and aspirations, then translate that information into a building that will instill pride of place. Here, architects discover they have many masters: those who pay for a government center, those who work there, live nearby, and visit the place for everything from food assistance to a marriage license. It is in this realm that those who have made public architecture their life's work learn to be patient, to focus on the important elements, and ignore the daily chatter.

Fentress has made public architecture his area of expertise, including government buildings that dig deep into a site's context and a community's cultures. This immersion is not confined to construction materials and social morés. The studio is intent on getting inside the community's heart, to create a building that will unify residents of all backgrounds.

The Clark County Government Center is mere minutes from the bright lights of the Las Vegas Strip, but that was the last image residents wanted for a complex that represented the way they lived. So the studio turned to the natural beauty of the region, where fire-red stone and vestiges of past cultures create an atmosphere layered with mystery. The voice of the ancient ones has been translated into a complex built for tomorrow.

CIVIC + GOVERNMENT

In Jefferson County, officials wanted to bring scattered services together on one site everyone could find, a beacon for residents of a sprawling mix of urban and mountain communities. In the process, Fentress referenced the colors of the surrounding landscape to integrate the appearance of both a government center and a human services building. The concept of welcome runs through these projects, from form to intent.

The City of Oakland was greatly damaged by the 1989 Loma Prieta earthquake, its downtown and civic complex ruptured and in need of both physical and psychological repair during a trying time. To weave the fabric of Oakland back together, Fentress devised a way to meld the look of new buildings and restored historic structures so that all eras were shown respect. The new civic complex helped mend the city, linked by a new plaza and pedestrian mall that make downtown a vibrant place.

Oakland was the first of several civic buildings for communities in California that Fentress designed.

In Sacramento, Fentress also faced the challenge of addressing a much-loved historic civic building to give officials room to grow and provide state-of-the art technology. The new Sacramento City Hall,

with its clean lines and contemporary materials, has helped solidify a key downtown block by reaching out to the old building, removing unsympathetic additions, and incorporating a nearby park.

The San Joaquin County Administration Building, in Stockton, California, consolidated more than a dozen agencies in a central location downtown. Finding this building is no problem: the Fentress studio designed an angular glass entry and atrium that explodes like a shard of mineral poking out of the earth. In this instance, though, this eye-catching formation is attached to a building that emulates the scale and rhythm of the neighboring historic buildings while referencing their designs in a contemporary manner. It is one-stop shopping, with a blast of color.

Long before sustainability standards were codified into the LEED rating system avidly followed today, Fentress pioneered innovative practices and materials for the Natural Resources Building in Olympia, Washington. Along with numerous techniques that battled the then-prevalent sick-building syndrome, the studio utilized the site and building to link other structures in the Washington State Capitol campus with nearby neighborhoods.

CLARK COUNTY GOVERNMENT CENTER

Location **Las Vegas, Nevada**
Client **Clark County General Services Department, Las Vegas**
Year **1995**

Curtis Fentress "There are public concerts outside. It's terrific. For an architect, this is an emotional moment. When you see people having a good time in your building, it is a thrill."

1

Clark County, Nevada, may be known for the bright lights, exotic architecture, and fast living of Las Vegas, its biggest city and a top-tier tourist destination. But one of the nation's biggest counties also includes stunning scenery, alluring recreational opportunities, and residential neighborhoods, all managed by a government that needed to consolidate services scattered throughout the area. In the process of building a new government center, the county confronted and confirmed its identity.

Fentress was awarded first place in a national competition for the new Clark County Government Center by immersing the studio in the area's culture and context. Yes, The Strip is a major player in terms of economic development, while offering fodder for commercials and gossip. But for the people who live and work in Clark County — the teachers, postal workers, fire fighters, business owners, and everyone else — it is home.

"We saw the county as the context," says Curtis Fentress. "We explored the natural areas. We hiked the trails. We visited Valley of Fire State Park, with its massive red sandstone formations, petroglyphs, and Mouse's Tank, a rock basin that collects rainwater and that got its name from an Indian who used to hide out there years ago. It's an interesting place. We skipped over The Strip, which is a mile or two away."

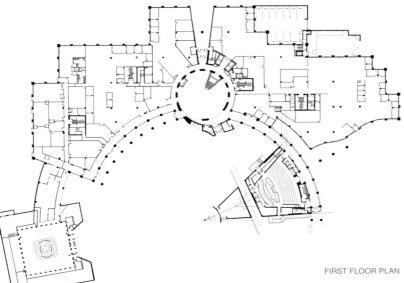

FIRST FLOOR PLAN

The Clark County Government Center draws from native forms, including the nearby sand dunes that informed the buildings' shapes. The center creates a natural curve around an outdoor space for public gatherings, referencing the idea of a government of the people.

An allée of trees helps form a spine that connects the government center with the nearby Regional Transportation Center/Regional Flood Control District Headquarters. Both share materials, forms and inspirations found in Clark County's scenic surroundings (following spread).

In a building designed for the public, Fentress looks for a key design principle to discover the natural order in the project. His master plan focused on a "spine" marked by an allée of trees, which connects the government center with Fentress' Regional Transportation Center/Regional Flood Control District Headquarters.

"One of the things important in designing a civic building is giving it a civic character, providing an organizing element to a big blank piece of ground," Fentress says. "The allée of trees is a big civic gesture, a way to attach other elements to the building. It's in the style of the Mall in Washington, D.C., and the Champs Elysées in Paris."

On one side of the allée, Fentress kept the land natural, using a circle as a way to organize the landscape and provide a focal point for the government center; on the other side is parking. County officials asked the studio four years later to return and design the Regional Transportation Center/Regional Flood Control District Headquarters, which has a similar wall system, uses the same stone, and offers the same organic feeling of a desert wash.

"We were able to create a sense of place that echoes the natural environment of Clark County and distinguishes the government center from the commercial district of Las Vegas," says Ned Kirschbaum, Fentress' principal and technical design director, who was project architect on the government center.

Calling the project "the highlight of my career," Kirschbaum says, "We gave the people of Clark County a special symbol of beauty that reflects where they live. The rotunda creates a sense of arrival and a play of light and stone you get when you hike in the mountains. The light splashes through."

The materials and design of both structures borrow from the most dramatic aspects of the region: sandstone walls, unexpected openings and details, and geometric shapes such as the government center's conical entry lobby and a pyramid topping an employee cafeteria, where custom-designed light fixtures feature upside-down pyramid-shaped shades.

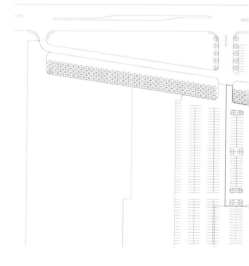

Carefully positioned windows and the atrium skylight provide natural light, accenting the sense of transparency of government, while areas most frequently visited by the public are on the lower levels and easy to find. An arcade screens visitors from the sun, while an amphitheater offers a gathering place for employees and the community.

"At a meeting for firms entering the competition, people got up and talked about what they wanted to see," says Fentress. "They mainly talked about the fact that the people of Las Vegas and Clark County lead normal lives, and they wanted a project that reflected the community. Las Vegas is not just The Strip. It's people going about their lives every day."

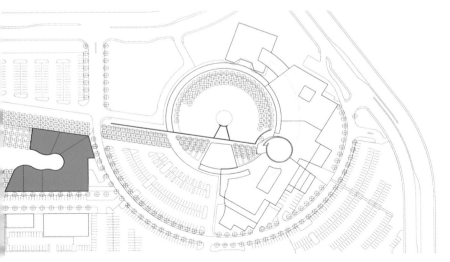

SITE PLAN

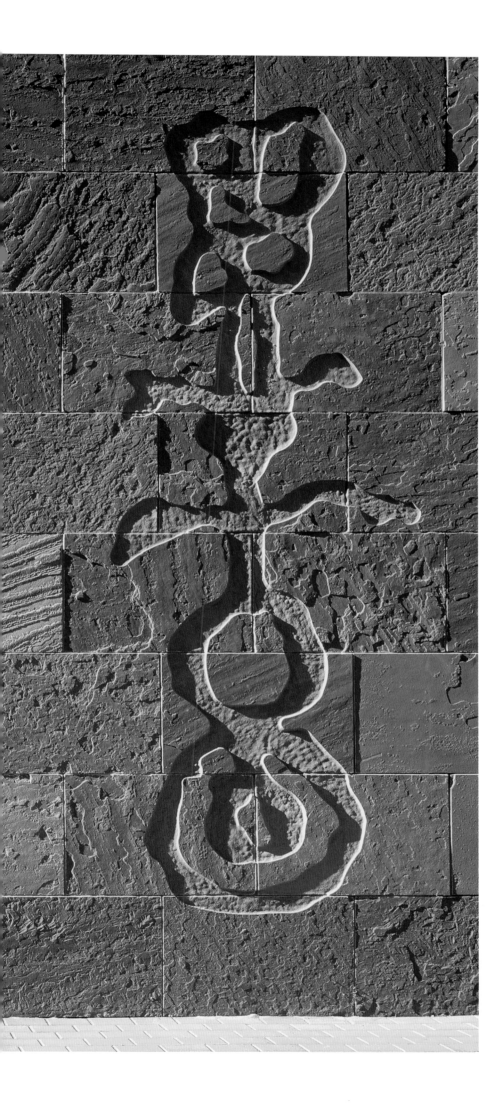

The petroglyphs of Valley of Fire State Park and other recreational sites found a way into details in the government center, which frames views that synthesize the manmade and the natural.

ROTUNDA SKETCH

Clark County is a hot, dry place, but healthful daylighting is an element in all Fentress designs. The stone interior of the government center's rotunda allows controlled light inside through carefully placed windows and a patterned skylight, making the entry a cool and welcoming place for the public (facing page).

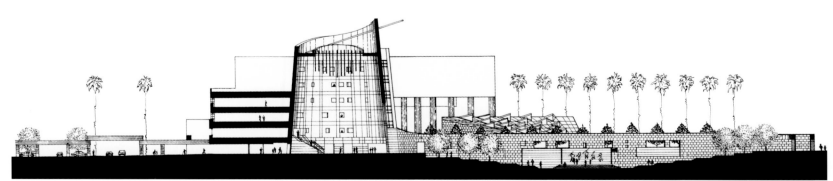

SECTION

EARTH ON FIRE

Valley of Fire State Park is located only about 55 miles away from Las Vegas, but it calls out to another time. The park's vibrant display of sculptural red sandstone formations was born 150 million years ago, producing an otherworldly valley of beauty that helped influence the design of the Clark County Government Center. The blazing color of the park's rocks, the geometric forms, the interplay of light and shadow, and the sense of being the bedrock of the West were translated into a set of modern buildings, a hub of civic activity in today's Nevada.

Near Lake Mead, Valley of Fire State Park was dedicated in 1935 and encompasses almost 36,000 acres of land. Though open for hiking and camping — and the occasional commercial or film shoot — Valley of Fire maintains the solitary elegance of a site that can influence architects seeking contextual power. The natural basin, dubbed Mouse's Tank, a collector for water after scant rainfalls, helped shape the cone-like rotunda at the government center, where civic responsibility to county residents is preserved and protected.

JEFFERSON COUNTY GOVERNMENT CENTER

Location **Golden, Colorado**
Client **Jefferson County, Colorado**
Year **1993**

Curtis Fentress "The Jefferson County Government Center is like a lantern on the landscape, signaling the most important building in the county. It is a freeway building, one you can see from busy Highway 6. You can look down through the valley, and see it."

Jefferson County sits to the west of Denver – a long, skinny county that wears two different hats. Jeffco is home to several cities, including Lakewood, Golden and Arvada, places settled during the rush to find gold in the Rockies. But the county also climbs up and around foothills and mountains, from the gentle hogback to the more rugged terrain of Mount Vernon and Deer Creek canyons.

For a citizenry with disparate needs and backgrounds, county officials wanted to corral scattered services under one, big domed roof, located near major thoroughfares: U.S. Highway 6 and 40, which link Denver to the mountains to the west, and E-470, which connects Highway 6 to the county's fast-growing suburbs to the southwest.

The result is the Jefferson County Government Center, which houses numerous public agencies as well as county court facilities, all in a distinctive yet easy-to-navigate building that separates these two vital civic functions while providing a large front door that signals accessibility.

"This building is about celebrating the entry," says Curtis Fentress. "We were selected to do the courthouse, but then officials changed the program to add the county agencies. The need for a central entryway led us to design a light-filled atrium that is more than 130 feet tall and easily visible from the highway, like a lighthouse that beckons people to safe harbor. The two arcs of the building even look like outstretched arms, welcoming and protecting its citizens."

The Jefferson County Government Center sits on open space at the foot of the Rocky Mountains, highly visible to the people who live in both urban and rural areas.

The government center's domed atrium is more than an entryway. It organizes and links the wings, informs the design of the sun-filled lobby, and shines like a beacon for people living in Jefferson County (following spread).

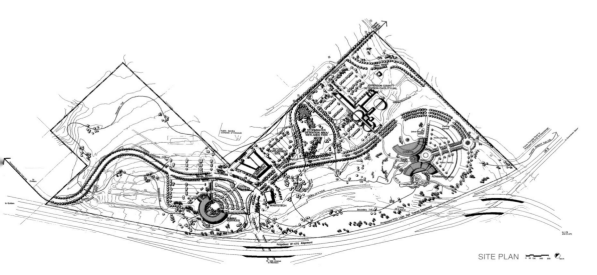

SITE PLAN

This split into two different functions – symbolized by two "wings" that reach out in an embrace – also required Fentress to devise a more thorough system for circulation and security. The studio became an early leader in providing protected passage for the different groups of people who participate in the justice system.

The courts are connected to a nearby jail by an underground tunnel, allowing prisoners to be transported in a secure manner to holding cells below the courthouse, where the incarcerated wait to be summoned to trial. A second circulation pattern for judges and court staff offers secure parking and entry to the courts area. Finally, the public enters through the main door, through security check points and to the courtrooms. Courts that serve a larger number of cases are on the ground floor, along with rooms where potential jurors wait to be called upstairs for trials that require juries.

Those headed to the administrative wing proceed in a different direction, to an area that houses offices for county commissioners and agencies, and conference rooms.

The government center grew out of two earlier Fentress projects for the county: the circular Human Services Building and a master plan designed to more fully define the large tract of open land being set aside for the county's civic facilities.

Both projects have succeeded in bringing agencies together under one roof: one-stop centers to serve the public, unify the county, and establish a strong presence, using colors borrowed from the landscape.

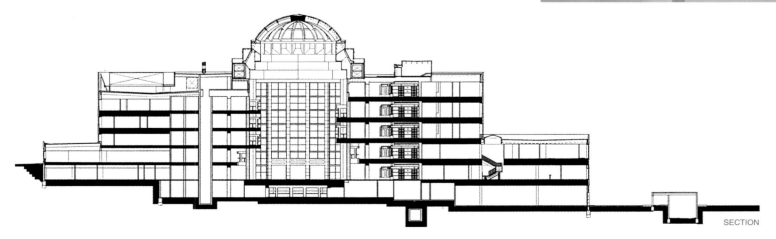

SECTION

A NATIONAL NAME

Thomas Jefferson's legacy lives long after his terms as president, vice president, secretary of state, and ambassador to France. His backing of the Lewis and Clark expedition of 1804, prowess in education and invention, and the great national expansion from the Louisiana Purchase of 1803 have earned him a giant stake in the country's cultural memory.

More than half the states in the United States include a Jefferson County, and Colorado is among them. The Centennial State's Jefferson County is one of the 17 original counties founded in 1861 by the fledgling Colorado Territory. This long and narrow county ranges from urban to nearly wild, challenging officials to maintain a steady and open government in diverse settings and among vastly different population centers. The need to consolidate public services and courts in one high-visibility location prompted construction of both the Jefferson County Human Services Building and the Jefferson County Government Center.

Location **Golden, Colorado**
Client **Jefferson County, Colorado**
Year **1989**

3

The Jefferson County Human Services Building reaches out to people who need support, through the courtyard for family visits and the sweeping glass solarium that allows daylight to flood the building.

Jefferson County took its first step to consolidate public services by selecting Fentress to design the Human Services Building and, later, to create a master plan to better utilize a large swath of open land earmarked for county agencies.

The building, constructed of bricks specially cast for circular walls, fronts on open space designed to welcome those seeking help – never an easy prospect.

"The Jefferson County Human Services Building was designed to be a calm place," says Curtis Fentress. "We did small things you wouldn't ordinarily think of. There is a courtyard that has a park-like feel, and the design allows the building to be light and airy. Part of public architecture is trying to take care of the most challenging situation in a humane way so people feel good, and to be humanistic so a place doesn't feel hard, institutional and difficult."

After the human services building proved successful at bringing various agencies together under one roof, Fentress' master plan identified a location for county courts and administration, a facility that also united far-flung functions to make life easier for Jefferson County residents.

Location **Oakland, California**
Client **City of Oakland**
Year **1998**

Curtis Fentress "Oakland, and many parts of the Bay Area, had suffered terrible damage in the 1989 Loma Prieta earthquake. For Oakland's administration buildings, we needed to look at the historic context and re-weave the fabric of a vibrant community, which had been torn like a piece of cloth. We were dealing with repairing and restoring historic civic buildings, while adding a new building and a plaza. Both old and new, every building has to celebrate the entry. It must be easy to understand and easy to navigate. It must have civic presence."

Millions of eyes were on the Bay Area the night of October 17, 1989. It was Game Three of a World Series that pitted the Oakland Angels and the San Francisco Giants in a contest fans dubbed the Battle of the Bay Bridge.

But when the ground began to shake at Candlestick Park, and the cameras bounced around like toy boats in a bathtub, one thing was painfully clear: people were watching an earthquake in action, until the lights went out. This surreal scene was like a movie, with Godzilla on a rampage, shaking and flattening buildings, cracking roads, and twisting bridges, including the crucial San Francisco Bay Bridge. The Loma Prieta quake eventually would kill over 60 people and injure thousands more, and leave hundreds of buildings damaged or unusable in the Bay Area.

That included a large part of Oakland, where civic and commercial buildings and homes were sent swaying, leaving many in need of attention, including the elegant, historic Beaux-Arts City Hall. City officials moved forward to not just repair and strengthen the existing buildings, but to reconnect civic structures, expand office space, and re-energize downtown with an updated plaza and retail opportunities.

The City of Oakland held a national competition to mend its heart and create a coherent government center. Fentress Architects was chosen unanimously, based on the studio's understanding of incorporating new buildings into a historic setting and its strength in designing for energy efficiency and a healthy indoor office environment.

Oakland's civic center revolves around the historic City Hall, the building at the bottom center of the aerial photo. Fentress' new Dalziel Building is to the left of City Hall. The Lionel J. Wilson Building, which expanded the old Broadway Building, is to the top right. The complex is tied together by the colorful Frank H. Ogawa Plaza. The plaza is the heart of the center and offers access to a highly prized Oakland Oak (following spread).

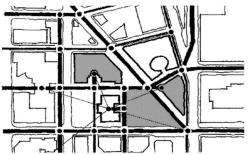

LINKAGE DIAGRAM

"We decided our best approach was to let context be our guide here, and work with the fabric of the historic buildings in the community," says Curtis Fentress. "From the City Hall to the Broadway Building, we analyzed the façades of those buildings to find the secrets of the cornice lines, the punch windows and the decorations. What did they have in common? We wanted to find a vocabulary to tie the new buildings to the historic, so when you looked at the new buildings, you would realize they were not from 1900 or 1920, but of a different time. Our time. And yet they were at home."

The first step was to stabilize the highly decorative historic tower of the 1914 City Hall; this crucial structure was placed on base isolation pads, then repaired and restored, a project completed by MWA Architects and VBN Architects.

The Fentress studio then approached what was then called the Broadway Building, later renamed the Lionel J. Wilson Building. This landmark structure needed seismic retrofitting, which included bracing the frame as well as anchoring the pieces of its terra cotta façade for safety and preservation. The studio also added on to the Wilson Building, extending the line with windows and cornices that reference the historic structure but pull from a different materials palette. For instance, the design incorporated metal rods to express the cornice line in a new section that reflected the scale and massing of the old. Fentress worked in conjunction with Muller & Caulfield Architects and Gerson Overstreet Architects.

A new office building across from City Hall, the Dalziel Building, is a rectangular block with one corner snipped off by a diagonal street. As the final piece of the puzzle, the city expanded an existing plan for the Frank H. Ogawa Plaza, designed by Y.H. Lee, adding green open space to the assemblage of civic structures to bring buildings – and citizens – together in a government center. Underground parking and ground-level retail were added to the mix.

In the process, the studio put the accent on easy-to-find entrances and interiors that were simple and intuitive to navigate. The Wilson Building was gutted, and turned into a modern office building. A main corridor through the building became a spine through the expanded structure; the studio retained as many doors, clerestories and walls as could work in a contemporary office setting. "A lot of the walls were shear walls, constructed out of cast iron, and there was a lot of terra cotta and masonry. It had wood floors. We had been doing a lot of renovation work, but this challenged and greatly expanded our repertoire of knowledge of old buildings."

To complete the package, streets between the Dalziel Building and City Hall, and between City Hall and the Wilson Building, were turned into pedestrian malls, and a large circular plaza was extended from City Hall. There stands one of the famed "Oakland oaks," brought back to prominence and health, a symbol of a city that has done the very same thing.

The cornice line of the new section of the Lionel J. Wilson Building follows the scale of the original structure, but uses a modern materials palette for expression (facing page).

The stylized entry of the Wilson Building frames views of the Beaux-Arts City Hall.

WILSON SIDE SECTION

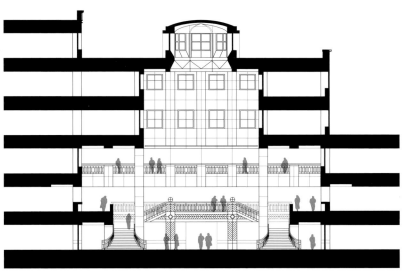

DALZIEL SIDE SECTION

The new Dalziel Building's entrance (left) presents a sleek, contemporary counterpoint to the more ornate City Hall.

The entry lobby of the Dalziel Building offers visitors sunlight and easy navigation to find city services.

THE MIGHTY OAK

Many cities bear the names of famous people, politicians, generals, movie stars. Oakland's heritage is a bit more basic: California's oak groves were especially plentiful in this area near the Bay, and from that tree "Oakland" was born. After the 1906 earthquake, those oaks helped rebuild San Francisco, which had been badly damaged by fire and seismic activity. Over the years, development and urban sprawl have taken a toll on the Oakland oaks. Those that remain now are revered members of the community. That includes an historic oak showcased outside Oakland's historic City Hall. To bring the oak into the new civic buildings that form the expanded civic complex, an abstracted version of an oak was woven into the ceiling of the Dalziel Building's lobby. Now a protected tree, the oak lives on in Oakland.

Location **Sacramento, California**
Client **City of Sacramento**
Year **2005**

Curtis Fentress "We approached the new Sacramento City Hall as a counterpoint to the original landmark building. There are even floor-to-ceiling windows so you can see into the city council chamber, signifying open and accessible government."

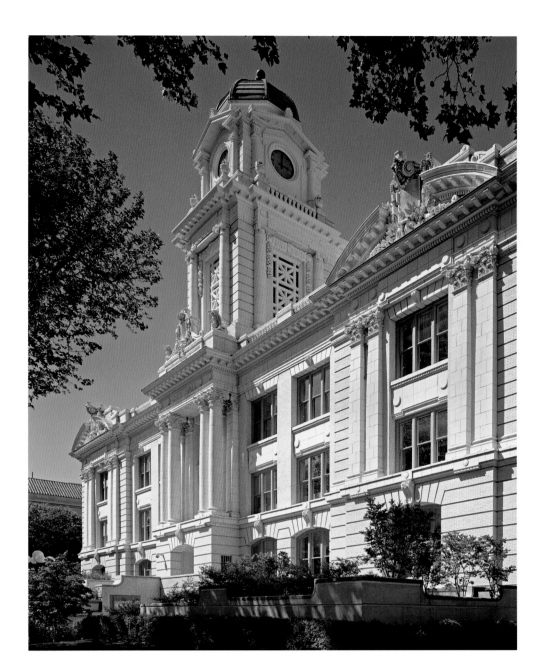

ELEVATION

A section drawing of the new Sacramento City Hall next to the historic city hall indicates references to massing, and deference to height.

When an architect is asked to build next to an exceptional historic structure in the capital city of California, the best thing to do is allow the older building to grab the spotlight – especially when it is a 1909 terra cotta and brick structure that looks as if it should be sitting on a table at a wedding reception.

But because that building, by noted California architect Rudolph Herold, is so small that many city services wind up scattered, officials decided it was time to add a modern space that could consolidate city agencies. Fentress' design for a new City Hall gave them a sophisticated, formalist building whose clean lines gently reach out to the old city hall, but never touch it.

Instead, Fentress removed two structures that abutted the old City Hall, clearing a respectful space around it and performing seismic upgrades to help the building thrive for another century. The new building, with parking below, also incorporates the existing César Chávez Park into the complex, showcasing open space on one of Sacramento's most prominent blocks. The scale of the new building reflects the old, while a façade of sleek windows focuses on the historic structure.

"Pushing a building against the City Hall didn't seem appropriate," Fentress says. "So we removed two old buildings, restored areas that had been disrupted by those connections, and left the old building to be a jewel unto itself. We left the corners of City Hall open and landscaped them to bring the green space behind City Hall, then

The arching façade of the new City Hall appears to embrace both the original building and César Chavez Park in the next block, creating a natural flow and completing a civic mall for Sacramento with the State Capitol Building as the other bookend.

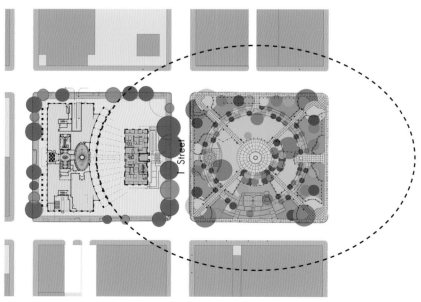

SITE PLAN

arched the building so it embraced the historic building. We created an arcade along the front of the new building to offer some relief from the sun and establish civic character. Basically, we set off the historic building, a grand piece of baroque architecture that's like loud organ music. The new building sits back from it, and lets it be."

The new City Hall is firmly rooted in public service. The city council chamber is on the ground level, making it convenient for the public. The mayor and city council have offices on the top floor, giving them a clear view of both the historic tower and the California State Capitol. The new building uses transparent glass, as a gesture toward the same material in the historic building but also to allude to transparency in government. And the new building is equipped to handle the 21st-century technology the old City Hall could not. Meanwhile, the old city council chamber is maintained as a ceremonial space.

In essence, this pairing of old and new, in its park-like setting, welcomes citizens and the business of government. "We used granite at the base and then brick above, in consideration of both the design and daily maintenance."

Formalist lines and sleek fenestration are hallmarks of the new City Hall, which focuses its attention on the ornate landmark building.

Location **Olympia, Washington**
Client **State of Washington, General Services Administration**
Year **1992**

6

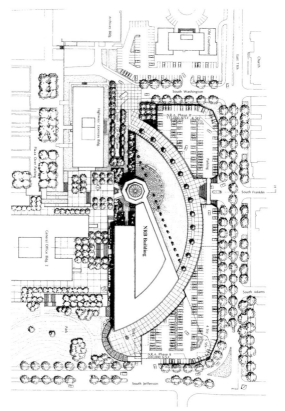

SITE PLAN

The site plan for the Natural Resources Building shows how the long, curved façade helps link the Washington State Capitol's campus to a nearby neighborhood, and serve as a bridge between architectural styles and eras, as well as uses.

The Natural Resources and Laboratories Building on the Capitol campus in Olympia, Washington, is a building designed to answer numerous needs. It is an early example of a building with strict sustainability standards met by strategies carefully developed by Fentress. It also is a crucial link between a historic government center and nearby mid-century residential neighborhoods.

The State of Washington and General Services Administration selected Fentress for the project during a national design competition for an office building that consolidates space for the state's departments of fisheries, agriculture and natural resources. But the structure also needed to anchor a new section of the campus, connect it visually with the original state complex and imposing Beaux-Arts Capitol Building, offer both a sense of openness and of enclosure with an arcade supported by a series of tree-like columns, oh, and be a good neighbor.

Fentress' master plan for the site resulted in a sweeping 675-foot-long façade that helps attach the cantilevered building to two worlds, with a light-filled rotunda that gives the building a focal point, a personality, and an easy-to-use space for public services.

When green was still just a color, strategies and materials used in the building near the Washington State Capitol aimed to produce a healthy workplace, with abundant daylight, energy conservation, and links to the outdoors.

"We had inherited a corner site that was an anchor for the campus," says Curtis Fentress. "We had the old and the new. We had height restrictions to preserve the view. The buildings there were an organizing element, and this long curvature tied it to the rest of the campus."

This "cornerstone" building also placed Fentress in a pioneering position in terms of sustainability. During this era, builders and health care professionals were concerned about what was termed the "sick building syndrome," where windows didn't open, air circulation systems lacked capacity, and the furnishings and finishes emitted noxious gases. The standards set by Fentress and regulatory agencies were designed to end the resulting headaches and other maladies with a very simple thing: fresh air.

"We did a lot of research on this project, and developed specifications that were more stringent in terms of testing materials used in the building so they were not off-gassing," Fentress says. In this era long before green, Fentress made a statement about bringing health back to the workplace.

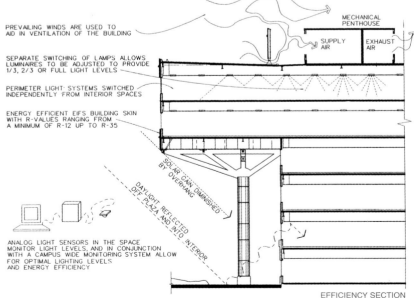

PREVAILING WINDS ARE USED TO AID IN VENTILATION OF THE BUILDING

MECHANICAL PENTHOUSE

SUPPLY AIR

EXHAUST AIR

SEPARATE SWITCHING OF LAMPS ALLOWS LUMINAIRES TO BE ADJUSTED TO PROVIDE 1/3, 2/3 OR FULL LIGHT LEVELS

PERIMETER LIGHT SYSTEMS SWITCHED INDEPENDENTLY FROM INTERIOR SPACES

ENERGY EFFICIENT EIFS BUILDING SKIN WITH R-VALUES RANGING FROM A MINIMUM OF R-12 UP TO R-35

SOLAR GAIN DIMINISHED BY OVERHANG

DAYLIGHT REFLECTED OFF PLAZA AND INTO INTERIOR

ANALOG LIGHT SENSORS IN THE SPACE MONITOR LIGHT LEVELS, AND IN CONJUNCTION WITH A CAMPUS WIDE MONITORING SYSTEM ALLOW FOR OPTIMAL LIGHTING LEVELS AND ENERGY EFFICIENCY

EFFICIENCY SECTION

SAN JOAQUIN COUNTY ADMINISTRATION BUILDING

Location **Stockton, California**
Client **San Joaquin County**
Year **2009**

Curtis Fentress   "San Joaquin County needed more than a new building. It needed greater efficiency, consolidating numerous departments to better serve the public and save money through sustainable building practices. Rather than move to the suburbs, officials decided to remain in historic downtown Stockton, with an eye toward boosting redevelopment efforts while demonstrating the transparent qualities of government."

7

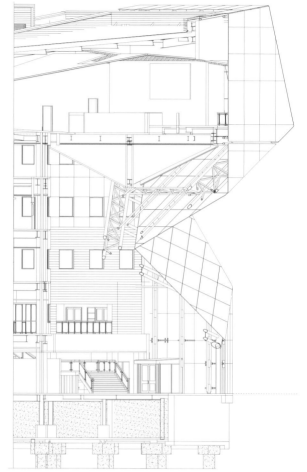

ATRIUM SECTION

The atrium's complex structural support system appears to double back on itself in order to carry the weight of several stories of green glass.

As winner of a design competition for a project that was intended as both shot in the arm and celebration of site, Fentress responded by giving the new San Joaquin County Administration Building a bold display of glass, a sparkling atrium that marks the building's entry and references nearby natural wonders such as Yosemite National Park. The sophisticated structural system that supports the glass allows passersby to see activity inside, while sustainable strategies have earned the project LEED Gold certification by the U.S. Green Building Council.

"They wanted to have their county commissioners' chamber on the top floor of the building, in view of the waterway that makes Stockton an inland port," says Curtis Fentress. "It is a symbolic connection with that trade route to the ocean 200 miles away. You can see ships docked here. The atrium is a big, green burst of glass, inspired by a piece of ore coming out of a mountain in the county, creating transparency of government."

Stockton's location in California's fertile delta and its role as a hub of maritime trade were not the only prompts for the design of a building that covers most of a city block. The old buildings downtown are built on narrow lots, setting up a dense pattern of windows, cornices and entries that defines the area's scale.

Fentress took a cue from this rhythm, breaking up the impact of the building's façade while tying the structure together through its massing and materials. The building's clean lines complement these historic neighbors, but also allow the atrium's unexpected flash of color to set off a building that is easy to find – an understatement, indeed.

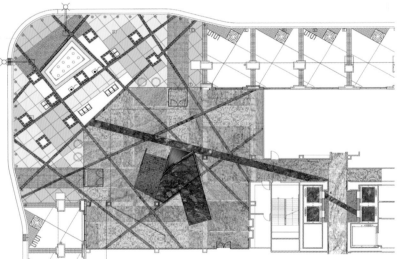

MATERIALS FLOOR PLAN

The building's atrium is awash in daylight, revealing a granite floor in a pattern that recalls the county's strong agricultural community. Textured wooden walls offer a contrast to the sleek glass "crystal" that forms the entry (facing page).

Fentress took scale and massing cues from downtown Stockton's historic buildings for the new San Joaquin County Administration Building, establishing a rhythm and referential articulation in a finely detailed façade.

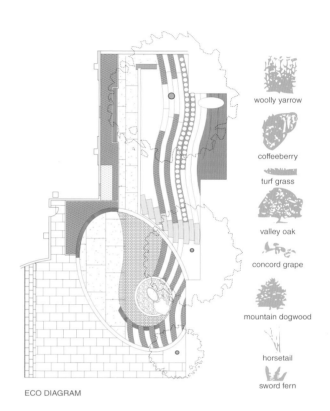

woolly yarrow

coffeeberry

turf grass

valley oak

concord grape

mountain dogwood

horsetail

sword fern

ECO DIAGRAM

Within sight of the California State Capitol, the state's Department of Education Headquarters is an early model of sustainable strategies. This includes an eco-park in which specific plantings such as woolly yarrow and sword fern attract beneficial insects to eat bad ones, a practice known as integrated pest management.

W hen it comes to sustainability, it helps to practice what you preach. For the State of California's Department of General Services, the goal for a new California Department of Education Headquarters in Sacramento was to achieve LEED Silver certification from the U.S. Green Building Council.

Instead, Fentress pushed to make this showpiece in the Capitol Area East End Complex a building ranked LEED 2.0 Gold. (Design architect on the project is Johnson Fain; Fentress is architect-of-record in association with Dreyfuss and Blackford Architects.)

The effort didn't stop there. Numerous sustainable strategies and materials – from high-tech to Old-World – led to the headquarters being recognized as the first state-owned building in the country to receive the council's LEED EB (Existing Building) Platinum certification.

"The architect, the client, the contractor, and the sub-contractors all wanted to set the example of a high standard in this area of sustainability," says Curtis Fentress. "Without everyone working together, you can't get there. It was a team effort. And the building performed so well we got Existing Building Platinum. That's a statement about the building. It wasn't just rated. It performed."

The team targeted sustainable design solutions inside and out: Fentress incorporated 110 green strategies into the project that save the state about $185,000 a year in maintenance expenses. The design team worked with carpet and acoustical ceiling manufacturers to remove formaldehydes and increase recycled content – products that were forward-thinking at the time, but are now considered standard in the industry. Solar panels were integrated into the building, and fly ash was mixed into the concrete. The landscape design includes on-site composters to recycle organic waste to use for soil enhancement. And an integrated pest management program eliminates the need for pesticides by specifying plant material that attracts beneficial insects, the types that eat bad bugs.

"My parents put praying mantises out in the gardens they planted after my father retired," says Fentress. "They ate bad bugs. That's the way people farmed. We're returning to some of the things that were done naturally in the past."

Discreetly installed solar panels help cut energy consumption but do not disrupt the sculptural presence of this high-performing building.

AND EARTH THAT I DESIRED TO LEARN

ED CARPENTER

Ed Carpenter works in a medium that is weightless and priceless.

Light.

After studying with European masters in stained glass, Carpenter recognized that what gave this historic medium its power was an element that surrounds us all. Carpenter, who works in large-scale sculptures and installations, found a material that can be shaped, manipulated and designed in a way that has an impact on a space, and on people.

"Light has the most emotional power when it is filtered, or reflected, or intensified by mediating elements," Carpenter writes, in the introduction to his 2000 book *Breath of Light*. "Furthermore, the affective qualities of light are accentuated by motion, the motion of the mediating elements, not the light itself."

Whether it is an exterior or interior sculptural installation or a bridge, Carpenter's designs are always different, rooted in the site, the context, the user and in a metaphor the artist finds during the development of the work. Just as Fentress designs one-of-a-kind buildings for each client, Carpenter seeks the unique quality, the appropriate solution, for art that can draw from the intangible but powerful force of memory. And just as Carpenter finds in light a basic element that can transform a space, Fentress uses light in his designs to symbolize the transparency of government and serve as a directional device in large public buildings such as airports.

"Sunlight can be felt to inflate and deflate a room as air would a lung, breathing vitality into it," says Carpenter, whose grandfather was a painter and stepfather an architect. "Understood in this way,

the manipulation of light in architecture becomes a game of layering and texturing, obscuring and revealing, and allowing the movement of shadows and light patterns to animate a room, a wall, or a courtyard. A building acts as the stable vessel into which sublime forces may be projected. Good architects understand all this."

Carpenter learned that stained glass basically was "bound to the wall," so that its "primary role in a building remains that of graphic membrane." He realized that buildings often were asking for more, seeking an intervention in the volume that involved engagement, spatial organization and excitement, and a way to evoke meaning in those who inhabited the space.

He searched for new materials and techniques, using the appropriate "toolkit" to accentuate what he calls the building's "sweet spot," the place where the light intersects.

Carpenter works in many different materials, including steel, copper, wood and fabric. But for projects where that "sweet spot" is elusive, he at times turns to a type of glass that can appear to be two colors at once, thus the name "dichroic."

Dichroic glass transmits about 50 percent of the light in a projection passing through the glass, and it reflects about 50 percent of the light in a reflection bouncing off the surface of the glass. The reflected color is the complement of the transmitted color. When the light hits the glass at an angle greater than 90 degrees or less than 90 degrees, there's a color shift. From one piece of glass, you have an opportunity to get different effects and different colors.

"The problem with dichroic glass is that it's such a strong material that when overused, it can be hideous. It's like certain musical instruments: You have to be careful not to be obtrusive."

Dichroic glass works like magic, seeming to find and amplify light in areas where the sun's rays are at a premium or coming together from different and changing directions. The kinetic aspects can involve architectural surfaces and thus magnify the influence of the work.

Carpenter studies potential sites to gauge their need for attention of some sort, with an eye toward making places memorable, habitable and human – just a few of the attributes that can prompt a sculptural intervention, or, in the case of a Fentress design, accentuate the public aspects of public architecture.

The third concept – human – is perhaps the most difficult to achieve. "I take very seriously the idea that what I create needs to be more than an assemblage of materials, more than good craft. It also needs to, or I want it to, stir something a little deeper than that. Public art for me works best if you can enter it first through the heart, then through the eyes, and then finally through the mind."

His installation for the expansion of Raleigh-Durham International Airport – *Triplet* – is a reference to Fentress' concept of an airport that draws from the region's high-tech universities, labs and industries, as well as North Carolina's long tradition of craft and artisanship. That is, mind-made and handmade.

Fabricated in tapered laminated wood masts with metal fittings, laminated glass and dichroic glass, *Triplet* is meant to serve as a marker, providing identification and orientation to the traveler. The "refined, hand-finished materials and fabrications are reminders of North Carolina's legacy of fine craft, and the triangular forms that the sculpture creates in space suggest the Research Triangle," Carpenter says. A separate way-finding sculpture, also in metal and glass, is designed to accentuate important signage.

"Curt's concept influenced me in designing the sculpture," Carpenter says. "It was an aid for a starting point for the sculpture. Although *Triplet* is initially and fundamentally a response to the volume of the space, the way it is fleshed out, the materials that were chosen, and the manner in which it is detailed come directly out of his thinking."

To connect RDU to the Carolina countryside, Fentress designed laminated Douglas fir beams that stretch almost 160 feet long, an innovative nod to the airport's context but also a forward-thinking strategy that required special testing to assure this material would stand up to potential extreme wind loads.

Carpenter, too, is always seeking new – and practical – ways of working.

"I'm always asking myself, 'What's the best way to do this? What's the most interesting way to do this? What's the most powerful way to do this?' " It's a combination of trying to find techniques that are expedient and ones that are fascinating, and both. At the same time, I find myself being drawn to certain materials or certain techniques repeatedly because they are the most expeditious."

They also seek out the heart of the sculpture.

"The very elemental qualities of sculpture, the timeless qualities that underpin all technology, are the foundation of everything we do. They're so reliable. Light and surface and form and texture: that's timeless. We can do a lot more with artificial light now because of new technologies, but it all needs to rest on a foundation of the elemental."

What is not immediate, or easy, or predictable, is Carpenter's exploration for a metaphor that both defines and strengthens his concept. It is a meander, not a straight line, and it is found in moments of solitude.

"I almost never start with the metaphor. I start with the physical condition of the space. Somewhere along the way, I find the metaphor. I come to understand that what I have been drawing, what I have been modeling, what I have been creating, reminds me of something. It will remind me of a thing, or of a quality, or of a part of biology that suddenly strikes me as appropriate to the client or to the site. It will be something beyond the physical part of the sculpture. I solve the physical problem first and then begin to understand the metaphor. In public art it's possible to work from the general to the specific. That's one way of ending up with something that has a chance of being appropriate in the space."

COURTS

7

RALPH L CARR COLORADO JUDICIAL CENTER
AL FARWANIA & AL JAHRA COURT COMPLEXES
NORFOLK CONSOLIDATED COURTS COMPLEX

COURTS

O ver many millennia, codes of conduct have becomes rules of law, setting down standards by which a people will comport themselves with an eye to fairness, harmony and equality.

To demonstrate the importance of the law and the legal system, architects have developed a vocabulary to inform the design of courthouses, to inspire dignity and respect toward the judicial system. Even as the law may change from city to city, or country to country, the form of buildings devoted to the legal system carries a special weight.

For Fentress, this means a heightened application of the studio's guiding principles, the Touchstones of Design. A courthouse must reflect the community's culture and context, and be organized for easy use by everyone from judges to court-watchers while stressing security, accommodating the needs of all who come before the court, and, in the end, serving as a place for people, where humanizing elements leaven the inherent monumentality of purpose. A courthouse is a civics lesson made real.

A project such as the Ralph L. Carr Colorado Judicial Center symbolizes the weight of a state's legal system. The courts – the third

branch of government – are embodied in buildings that do more than consolidate the state's supreme and appellate courts, and dozens of related offices and agencies. The Carr complex also includes the latest in technology, heightened but subtle security, flexibility for the future and, because of its site, respect for both the nearby Colorado State Capitol and the cherished political and cultural heart of the city: Denver's Civic Center. For Fentress, all buildings carry responsibility; a complex that represents his home state's legal system is a commission that bears a challenge and opportunity of the highest order.

The Fentress studio has become a leader in incorporating innovative sustainable practices and triple circulation systems that protect the public, the accused, and the judges and officers of the court. And as court records are being stored electronically and more evidence is presented in electronic form, Fentress' design incorporates innovative technology that is flexible and reliable in legal proceedings.

The Norfolk Consolidated Courts project carries an additional responsibility, that of helping to revitalize a downtown area in spirit and functionality. The introduction of light rail in this part of the city places this courts complex in the category of transit-oriented

development, where access and the relationship to other buildings takes on new importance. A project naturally woven into the city's core maintains a respectful attitude toward the legal system while making the facility part of the basic public realm.

Translating the studio's respect for courthouses into a location half-way around the world requires an even greater immersion in context and culture. Fentress won first prize in an international competition to create a series of courthouses in Kuwait by presenting concepts that stressed memorable aesthetic elements, intuitive yet secure circulation patterns, and sustainable strategies crafted to address intense climatic conditions. Though the buildings will share architectural gestures that signify courthouse status, each structure will relate to a specific site and the needs of the court system.

They are buildings designed to last. After all, people come and go, but the law continues.

Location **Denver, Colorado**
Client **State of Colorado**
Year **2013**

Curtis Fentress "For an architect devoted to designing public buildings, the opportunity to work on the most significant legal symbol for Colorado is a project of a lifetime. Courthouses, after all, are the visible manifestation of the American legal system, a core element in the interpretation and application of the law for all people. I'm trying to instill in the building the dignity of the courts and the importance of the third branch of government."

C ivic Center is Denver's heart, where government and culture meet in a historic Beaux-Arts setting that demonstrates the evolution of architectural style over the past century. But at its core, this park-like assemblage of buildings also serves as a metaphor for the promise inherent in a civic environment.

From the Colorado State Capitol to the library to the Denver Art Museum, this district pulls people bent on many missions and pleasures. After years of prodding by Denver Mayor Robert Speer to give Denver a civic center, most of planner Edward H. Bennett's 1917 scheme was realized, with an idealized sense of public service and the best in public architecture. It is, truly, a legacy of the City Beautiful movement.

Fentress won the design competition to add the latest – perhaps last – member of the Civic Center club, a courts complex that will not only be the state's largest law office but also a symbol of the Centennial State's third branch of government.

The new Ralph L. Carr Colorado Judicial Center, will house courtrooms for the Colorado Supreme Court and Colorado Appellate Court, consolidate numerous state legal offices, and anchor a crucial site on Denver's Civic Center.

The judicial center sits on a full city block next to the Colorado State Capitol. The domed, four-story Neoclassical courts building contains two courtrooms for the appellate court and one for the supreme court, offices for judges and justices, and service areas. These components cluster around a soaring atrium, with a glass span that fills the building with natural light and symbolizes transparency in the state's legal system. This giant glass "wall" is designed to make the joins close to invisible. A portion of the building is earmarked for an educational facility for students and adults. Its green roof is designed to frame a million-dollar view of the Capitol, while offering a visible link to the sustainable practices and materials being designed into the center.

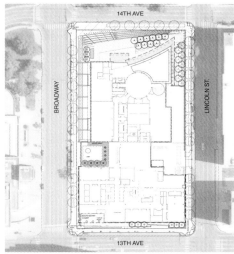

SITE PLAN

The ceremonial entry of the courthouse center is signaled by a portico, an architectural element important to the Neoclassical buildings of Denver's nearby Civic Center. The site plan of the buildings designed to house Colorado's state courts shows the link between the courts and office buildings as well as gestures that relate the judicial center to the Beaux-Arts Civic Center to the west.

For many people, the most notable element will be that entry, with its bold four-columned portico set on a curved walkway that forms a literal and gestural connection to Civic Center. The main entry is mostly ceremonial, but its impact will be felt beyond those who walk through the doors: it is positioned to be highly visible to the thousands of vehicles that drive by the Civic Center each day.

To the south, the 12-story office building presents a complementary, but more contemporary, design. The tower houses offices and service agencies, and will allow for flexibility and growth. The office building's design is more streamlined, although it still recalls Neoclassical elements, with a columned presence on the busy Broadway corridor. A corner entry and arcade relate to the newer portion of the Denver Central Library.

Both buildings will key off the rich gray granite of the nearby Capitol and share a rusticated granite base. The court building's exterior will be honed granite laid in a stacked running bond, while the office tower will be clad in articulated architectural precast colored to match or complement the Capitol's stone.

The design of a state court complex taps into every one of Fentress' guiding principles, The Eight Touchstones of Design. The circulation system must be intuitive, especially when dealing with security and public access, and the entrance easy to identify. All voices must be heard during the design process, to result in buildings that respect the cultures of Colorado and the spirit of the law. Finally, this must be a design for people – all people. The center must reflect honesty, gravity and strength, on a commanding site and carrying a name revered in Colorado.

"We've worked hours, late into the night, to decide how the lines should run through the building . . . how the domes will be expressed," says Curtis Fentress. "It all matters. We constantly have to remember why we're designing this building, and how to humanize it for those who will experience what it stands for. The bottom line is that simplicity always trumps confusion."

The glass dome of the courts building features glass walls with nearly invisible joins that afford sweeping views of the Colorado State Capitol Building (bottom right). The columns that mark the entry of the courts building and its innovative learning center are repeated in a more contemporary manner in the office tower (facing page).

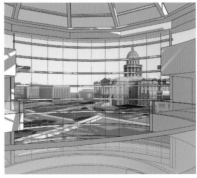

AL FARWANIA & AL JAHRA COURT COMPLEXES

Location   **Kuwait City, Kuwait**
Client   **Kuwait Ministry of Public Works | Kuwait Ministry of Justice**
Year   **2014**

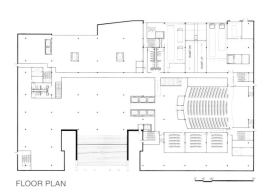

FLOOR PLAN

The design of court buildings for Kuwaiti governorates shares elements that can be adapted to the topography of different sites. Site plan keys in on the entry to the building and the circulation pattern of the first floor.

T he Kuwaiti court system may have complexities unique to that country, in terms of the court structure and the impact of religious law. But as public buildings, courthouses worldwide share the need to mix distinctive aesthetics with intuitive circulation and state-of-the-art security.

The Ministry of Justice in Kuwait led the design competition for the Al Farwania and Al Jahra Court Complexes, new facilities located in two of the nation's five governorates. Fentress' proposal was awarded first place for its innovative approaches to courthouse circulation, sustainability and the incorporation of modern technology. The design calls for 80 courtrooms per 16-story building, which share architectural gestures that can be adapted to the requirements of each site, remaining sensitive to context and culture. Fentress also has provided peer review and design assistance on a third courthouse, the 25-story Hawally Courts Complex.

As with all court projects, security is a key element, as important as designing a building that remains a place for people and the open expression of the law. Clear and safe circulation patterns are expressed in secure, restricted and public zones. Strategies contributing to a sustainable design include the use of "cool" roofs, photovoltaic panels and carefully placed sunshades.

The overall design will express stability, permanence, fairness and the importance of the law, along with the open and transparent judicial process at the heart of any courthouse.

"Our design is built around a civic atrium, and a symbolic civic entrance to the building," says Curtis Fentress. "A large glass wall will be detailed in a geometric pattern, shielding the sun, but allowing people to see inside and outside the building. This is part of our usual strategy to allow light in to every part of the building, including courtrooms."

The glass façade in the court building serves various functions. It includes a pattern that references regional cultural cues and symbolizes the transparency of the justice system at work.

West Elevation   South Elevation   East Elevation   North Elevation   North South Section   East West Section

NORFOLK CONSOLIDATED COURTS COMPLEX

Location **Norfolk, Virginia**
Client   **City of Norfolk**
Year   **Phase 1: 2013, Phase 2: 2014**

3

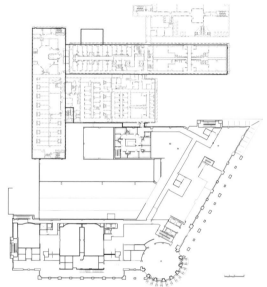

FLOOR PLAN

A domed atrium helps define the organization of the Norfolk Consolidated Courts Complex, where two "wings" set along major city streets offer easy access for those visiting.

N orfolk is an old city, a place defined as much by water as by history.

Early on, a strategic location on Chesapeake Bay turned this port city into a trading partner to the world and home to a significant U.S. military presence, with the U.S. Navy's largest installation in the nation.

But as the shipping industry changed, Norfolk turned its attention to revitalizing abandoned port facilities and a sagging downtown. A festival marketplace and maritime museum have created activity, but recharging the urban core remains a high priority.

To consolidate several courts and help focus the city's government complex, officials eyed a new courthouse at the heart of the Civic Center Plaza, where a city hall and courts facility were built almost half a century ago.

To bring order and vitality to this area, Norfolk officials selected Fentress to design a courthouse that consolidates and expands the courts while weaving itself into the downtown fabric. Phase 1 will house circuit and general district courts; Phase 2 will incorporate domestic relations and juvenile courts. At completion, the complex will include 24 courtrooms.

The new development will be adjacent to a light-rail station, connecting the courts to the city at large and helping to trigger redevelopment in the area. The courts complex is to be built in phases, eventually bringing all the city's judicial components under one roof (at right).

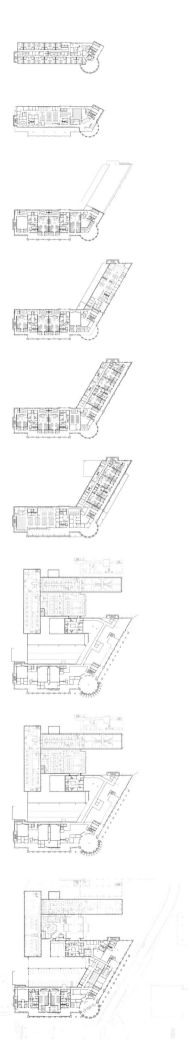

"They want a building that brings more cohesiveness to this major complex of civic buildings," says Curtis Fentress. "And they want to tie it to the light-rail station as a key transit-oriented development.

The new courthouse is sited on a busy intersection so its "wings" link two streets and give an edge to an expanded plaza. A domed, round tower with a light-filled atrium will serve as the "hinge" and focal point. Built of architectural precast, the new building will feature the three secure circulation systems that have made Fentress a leader in court design. And arcaded passageways and clear entries will welcome those seeking justice, sparking renewal in the process.

FLOOR PLANS

JESÚS MOROLES

Jesús Moroles has become one with stone, a material that for thousands of years has symbolized permanence, integrity and beauty.

Building in stone has become a gauge of how advanced a civilization is in terms of its tools, its artisans, its perception of time, and beauty. Stone also is a living thing, born of pressure and upheaval as the earth has changed and shifted over millions of years.

For Moroles, whose massive works span the globe and include large contemplative installations, only the toughest stone – granite – attracted his interest. This captivating material called to him partially because of its speckled splendor, and partially because of the challenge in pulling form from substance.

"There is beauty in marble, in travertine and other stones but granite. . . ," Moroles says, his voice trailing off. "When I got to granite, it is so consuming that it exhausts me. It is relentless. It is the challenge, but when you're finished, you have something that will outlast everything. It's permanent. It will be here long after we're gone. Marble and other

The concept of stone as a timeless medium in art finds a parallel in architecture, and certainly has found a voice in the work of Curtis Fentress. In museums, courthouses and convention centers, Fentress has employed stone as an emblem of stability and context. For the National Museum of Wildlife Art, for instance, rough stacked fieldstone walls meld with the site, a wild, scenic place that is the West at its natural best. For the design for the courts building of the Ralph L. Carr Colorado Judicial Complex, a subtle gray granite block complements the nearby Colorado State Capitol and Denver's historic Civic Center. And in the Palm Springs Convention Center, the organic shape of stone walls and imposing pylons recalls the mountains nearby.

"It's mainly about man and nature working together," Moroles says. "The stone itself is the starting point. Part of what I attempt to do with my sculpture is to bring the quarry into the gallery – to make the stone important by drawing attention to it, and to show the finished pieces as the result of an interaction between man and nature. I always choose pieces that can retain a suggestion of their original formation. By working in response to the character of the stone, I want to expose the truth of the material."

That quote dates from 1981, the beginning of the artist's formal career. After earning a bachelor of fine arts degree in 1978 from the University of North Texas, Denton, the Corpus Christi native worked for the late sculptor Luis Jiménez. "It was my graduate school," Moroles recalls. "Everything he was doing, I would be doing, except he was in fiberglass and figurative, and I was doing stonework and abstract forms."

This intense immersion in sculpture also gave Moroles a chance to save money to spend a year in Pietrasanta, Italy. There, he worked stone. He studied stone. He traveled to look at and touch stone. When he returned, he confronted granite. He became consumed, and even though at age 11 he had learned about hard work at his uncle's masonry firm, his education was about to escalate.

"I was working on my first piece of granite, and wearing all my protective gear, and finally I got so exhausted that I put down my tools. And when the dust settled, there were 30 people within four feet of me. I did not know anybody was there. I was lost in the work. That's when I realized there was some kind of a connection there. I was lost in it."

There's that mix of beauty and challenge again, where some of the appeal comes from how the stone is formed. "Granite doesn't have faults. Granite is igneous, the Latin for 'fire'. It is cooked, like porcelain. It comes from the center of the earth, by heat and pressure. That's why it's a super material. Marble is sedimentary, like other stones, and the layers of dirt have been pressed together. Water can dissolve it, and that's the difference between other stones and granite."

Granite also does not have faults, like other stones, but it has an attribute just as challenging, Moroles says. "There is a rift in granite, a vein. The way it's pushed up from the earth is the vein of the granite. When you carve it, and you're carving against the grain, it doesn't come off. And when you carve with the grain, it comes off a little bit. You want to go with the grain. But you don't know till you get in there."

For his sculptures and installations, Moroles selects his own blocks, attracted by the size, the vein, or the way the piece was torn out of the ground. "There's something about it. When you go to the beach, you don't bring all the shells back. You just bring one. There's something about that one shell you bring back. That's the starting place for me with a block of stone. It's already got me thinking about the possibilities."

To investigate the stone – and, ultimately, to change its shape and nature – Moroles will begin the process of tearing it open, using wedges to pry apart giant slabs to be carved, dressed, polished and textured, while leaving surfaces that revel purely in the act of being rough stone.

His studio assistants often will work on a piece without knowing what it is. "All my drawing for a sculpture is done on the stone. There are no sketches. The workers carve to that drawing. I look at it, and then I draw again. And they carve and polish that. I'm constantly looking at the pieces and drawing the next step. A collector asked one of my guys, 'What are you making?' and he said, 'I don't know.' He didn't know what he was making, because I didn't know either. It's just a process of steps. Every part of every piece is done by me. It's the only way I can keep my hands on it and keep control."

He has help, he says, because some of his larger sculptures — and, more recently, complete environments — require moving many pieces of granite around, with numerous steps needed to reveal the art inside. It is this same sort of patient search that fuels Fentress' approach to the design of a building, incorporating the wishes of those who will use the building, the natural demands of the site, the cultural milieu of the region, and the aim for timelessness in form and intent.

Moroles also faces the hazards of working with an unforgiving material, crawling on ladders and scaffolding, wielding heavy tools, and pushing and pulling mega-blocks of stone. He's a tall, robust man, but stone is heavy. It's a dangerous pursuit.

"I've almost died more than several times. Each time I feel I've gotten another chance and I come out working like a crazy maniac because I feel I've gotten another chance to do more work." On one project, he fell off the 30-foot-tall sculpture and couldn't walk for a year. Yet, "I'm still the first one to go up the scaffolding. I wouldn't ask any of the guys to do anything I wouldn't do. I'm the last one off the scaffolding. I'm afraid of heights because I fell off that first piece. But If I don't do it, I can't expect them to do it. I have to act like I'm not scared."

The Houston Police Memorial, 1992:
"Peter Marzio, director of the Museum of Fine Arts Houston, and Mrs. De Menil, from The Menil Collection, were on a committee doing an international search for an artist. Then they said, 'Let's invite someone locally,' and invited me. They showed me the place. I didn't answer them for a year. I didn't know if they had found somebody. I went to Europe to look at what makes people go to places, what makes places special. I went to Tibet to look at what makes sacred spaces.

"When I came back, I had an idea. I looked at the place. I decided I didn't want to bring anything to that place. I wanted to carve the place. I acted like I was the Jolly Green Giant, and I dug into the ground. It was clay. I dug holes, and what I took out I used to make a mound. Then I wanted to climb up and down, and that's how the terraces came about. It's the only ziggurat step pyramid in the world that is growing out of the ground. All the others are standing on the ground. The memorial is in the shape of a cross when you look down from the sky. So it has a lot of symbolism. I came up with something new. I wasn't trying to copy a pyramid. Because I'm a carver, I decided to carve the land."

Joslyn Art Museum, *The Omaha Riverscape*, **Nebraska, 2009:**
"Projects like this take three to five years. There are meetings with architects. You're doing stuff that's never been done before. Here, the fountain is pumping water and becoming a river and then a reflecting pool. In the wintertime, I hate fountains being off. So I put hot water lines under the river part of this piece, so there's never any snow on the river. The river is from the drawings the museum has of the Lewis and Clark expedition. It's the river that runs through Omaha to Sioux Falls through Plattsmouth. I used to live there when I was in the Air Force, at Offutt Air Force Base. I lived on the Platte River. I really had a connection with it. They showed me the project, and I did the drawing within 10 minutes of their telling me about it. They're walking me through the museum, and I've sketched it on a napkin. And we did it."

"When I was leaving Italy, to start my work, I went to the top of Mount Altissimo with a friend. It is this historic mountain, where Michelangelo found the purest marble in the world, to carve the **David.** *We went there early in the morning and started walking up, through the last village. At the top, I looked over and you could see the other side of the mountain, and see daybreak. Then we walked down that pathway that people have walked on for hundreds of years. I realized that I was stepping on footholds that were carved by man. The whole mountain is white marble. Where man had touched it, it was soft and molded by the footprints from shoes going over it for hundreds of years. Around it was rough, white stone, with grass growing. There was dew, so the stone was wet. When you wet marble, it looks like it's polished. Parts were rough, where man hadn't stepped on it. I said, 'If I could cut this step out, this is what I want my work to be like, where man has touched it but it still has the sense of where it came from. This is what I want to do.' I came back and did my first piece. It was titled* **Fountain,** *with granite, water and mirror-polish stainless steel – a mix of nature and man."*

8

EDUCATION + LABS

UNIVERSITY OF COLORADO DENVER RESEARCH 1 & 2
SANFORD CONSORTIUM FOR REGENERATIVE MEDICINE
DAVID E. SKAGGS FEDERAL BUILDING | NOAA HEADQUARTERS
UNIVERSITY OF COLORADO MATHEMATICS BUILDING AND GEMMILL ENGINEERING LIBRARY
UNIVERSITY OF CALIFORNIA | IRVINE HUMANITIES GATEWAY

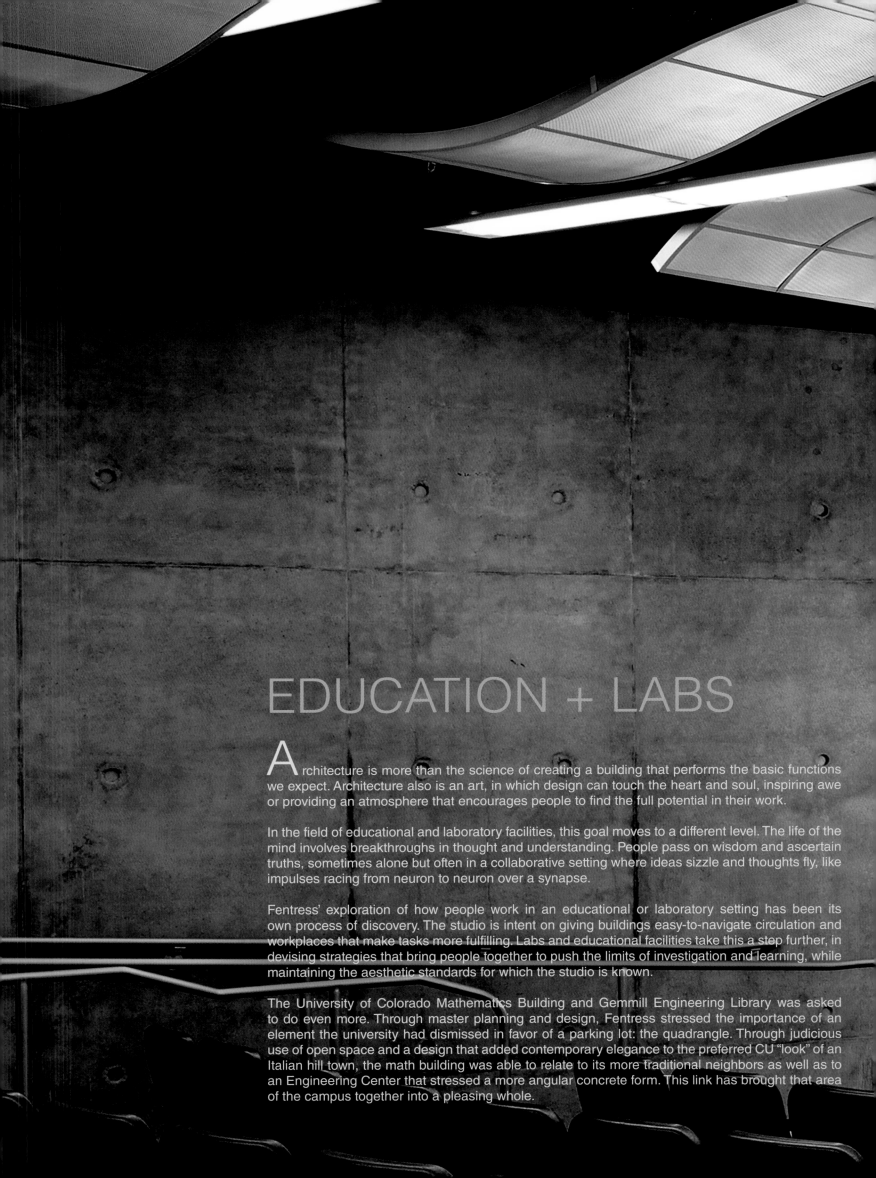

EDUCATION + LABS

Architecture is more than the science of creating a building that performs the basic functions we expect. Architecture also is an art, in which design can touch the heart and soul, inspiring awe or providing an atmosphere that encourages people to find the full potential in their work.

In the field of educational and laboratory facilities, this goal moves to a different level. The life of the mind involves breakthroughs in thought and understanding. People pass on wisdom and ascertain truths, sometimes alone but often in a collaborative setting where ideas sizzle and thoughts fly, like impulses racing from neuron to neuron over a synapse.

Fentress' exploration of how people work in an educational or laboratory setting has been its own process of discovery. The studio is intent on giving buildings easy-to-navigate circulation and workplaces that make tasks more fulfilling. Labs and educational facilities take this a step further, in devising strategies that bring people together to push the limits of investigation and learning, while maintaining the aesthetic standards for which the studio is known.

The University of Colorado Mathematics Building and Gemmill Engineering Library was asked to do even more. Through master planning and design, Fentress stressed the importance of an element the university had dismissed in favor of a parking lot: the quadrangle. Through judicious use of open space and a design that added contemporary elegance to the preferred CU "look" of an Italian hill town, the math building was able to relate to its more traditional neighbors as well as to an Engineering Center that stressed a more angular concrete form. This link has brought that area of the campus together into a pleasing whole.

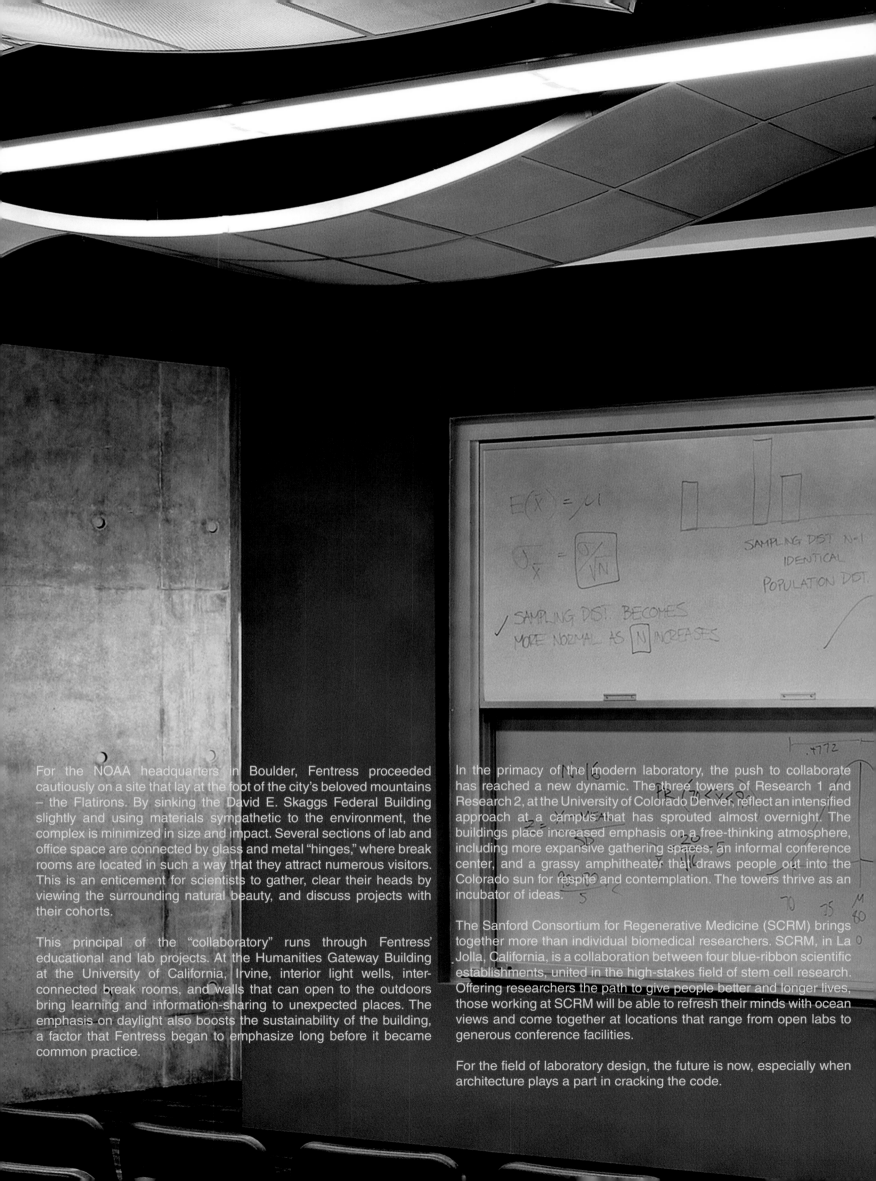

For the NOAA headquarters in Boulder, Fentress proceeded cautiously on a site that lay at the foot of the city's beloved mountains – the Flatirons. By sinking the David E. Skaggs Federal Building slightly and using materials sympathetic to the environment, the complex is minimized in size and impact. Several sections of lab and office space are connected by glass and metal "hinges," where break rooms are located in such a way that they attract numerous visitors. This is an enticement for scientists to gather, clear their heads by viewing the surrounding natural beauty, and discuss projects with their cohorts.

This principal of the "collaboratory" runs through Fentress' educational and lab projects. At the Humanities Gateway Building at the University of California, Irvine, interior light wells, inter-connected break rooms, and walls that can open to the outdoors bring learning and information-sharing to unexpected places. The emphasis on daylight also boosts the sustainability of the building, a factor that Fentress began to emphasize long before it became common practice.

In the primacy of the modern laboratory, the push to collaborate has reached a new dynamic. The three towers of Research 1 and Research 2, at the University of Colorado Denver, reflect an intensified approach at a campus that has sprouted almost overnight. The buildings place increased emphasis on a free-thinking atmosphere, including more expansive gathering spaces, an informal conference center, and a grassy amphitheater that draws people out into the Colorado sun for respite and contemplation. The towers thrive as an incubator of ideas.

The Sanford Consortium for Regenerative Medicine (SCRM) brings together more than individual biomedical researchers. SCRM, in La Jolla, California, is a collaboration between four blue-ribbon scientific establishments, united in the high-stakes field of stem cell research. Offering researchers the path to give people better and longer lives, those working at SCRM will be able to refresh their minds with ocean views and come together at locations that range from open labs to generous conference facilities.

For the field of laboratory design, the future is now, especially when architecture plays a part in cracking the code.

Location **Aurora, Colorado**
Client **University of Colorado Denver Health Sciences Center**
Year **2004, 2008**

Research 1 (above right) includes a double-decker bridge that links north and south towers to promote ease of movement and communication among researchers. Aerial view (above) spotlights the quadrangle, a welcomed gathering place for students and co-workers.

For years, the University of Colorado Denver Health Sciences Center wanted to leave its cramped site in the city. When the center finally moved, it was to an ensemble of new towers on a vast campus several miles east devoted to hospitals, clinics and medical research.

Almost overnight, a gleaming instant city emerged on a former Army hospital facility: the old Fitzsimons now sported buildings that hewed to a uniform materials palette; clean, contemporary lines, and placement on a grid that defined purposes such as treatment, education and research. Fentress, in association with KlingStubbins, is responsible for Research 1 and Research 2.

Research 1 was part of an early wave of construction there, and it reflected Fentress' belief in discovering the natural order through connecting the building's two towers and forming the beginnings of a quadrangle. When Research 2 joined the mix, it added to the assemblage by further defining a gathering space for students marked by a lawn and amphitheater.

Just as important was the emphasis on collaboration between researchers, giving them opportunities to reflect in a natural setting or bounce ideas off each other to further their knowledge and research. This building concept – a collaboratory – is evidenced at the research complexes by two-story break rooms, a two-level glass-clad covered bridge, auditoriums and conference rooms that form an informal conference center and natural magnet for relaxed discussion and synergistic thinking.

The campus-wide materials palette of brick and glass keeps the research buildings alive at night (facing page), while two-level break rooms and other connectors encourage the interaction that defines a collaboratory.

"The quadrangle gives it much more of a campus feeling," says Curtis Fentress. "Historically, this is where students would relax, sit on the grass, read a book, or talk with friends. This offers researchers the same kind of atmosphere for a communal educational space."

In both complexes, flexibility is built in to accommodate changing research needs over time. Yet the towers follow a similar organizational scheme, in which offices face into the courtyard/quadrangle and labs face out to views of the mountains and the prairie. Both the 9- and 12-story towers in Research 1 and the 11-story tower in Research 2 are clad in brick, with one side in blue-tinged glass and aluminum curtain walls.

"Just as there are design standards at the University of Colorado, the medical campus requires materials that relate to each other even though the buildings have different programs, functions, and architects," says Fentress. "The bricks and glass weave a fabric for the campus, so one vocabulary can result in many different expressions."

Top: Laurence Chan MD. D.Phil (Oxon) is Professor of Medicine and Director of Transplant Nephrology Research at the University of Colorado Denver. He received his medical training at the University of Hong Kong and the University of Edinburgh, as well as Oxford and Harvard. Dr. Chan is a pioneer in the early development of magnetic resonance in medicine and in the application of nuclear magnetic resonance related to cellular metabolism and transplantation. He is a founding member of the American Society of Transplant Physicians, a founding member of the Society of Magnetic Resonance in Medicine, and a co-founder and executive board member of the American Transplant Foundation.

Bottom: Dr. Richard J. Johnson is Temple Hoyne Buell and NKF of Colorado Endowed Professor of Medicine and Chief of the Division of Renal Disease and Hypertension at the University of Colorado Denver. Dr. Johnson received his undergraduate degree in anthropology in 1975 from the University of Wisconsin, and his M.D. in 1979 from the University of Minnesota. He joined the UCD faculty in 2008, and remains an Adjunct Professor of Medicine at the University of Florida. He is author of *The Sugar Fix* , which discusses the impact of fructose-containing sugars on overall health, and an editor of the popular textbook *Comprehensive Clinical Nephrology*.

"What I like about the Research Complex is the unique design of the buildings, centered on an open courtyard overlooked by corridors, offices, break rooms and laboratories. Well-positioned windows give plenty of light and views, including the Front Range. For a moment, I can almost feel that I'm back in Oxford with the buildings and quads designed by Sir Christopher Wren. The laboratory interiors are a dramatic departure from traditional labs, with open space and views. Shared instrumentation laboratories such as NMR (nuclear magnetic resonance) machines foster a spirit of openness and collaboration between scientists. The break rooms are well-positioned in different floors with easy access and connection by stairs. They act as a social magnet, encouraging informal meetings and chance encounters. It's a joy and a privilege to be able to work in this research complex."

"I was recruited to the University of Colorado in October of 2008 and was one of the first scientists to move into Research 2. The beautiful state-of-the-art laboratories with adjacent spacious offices were among the more attractive aspects of the recruitment. The building is perfectly suited for networking and collaborations, and its proximity to the University Hospital and to Children's Hospital is ideal."

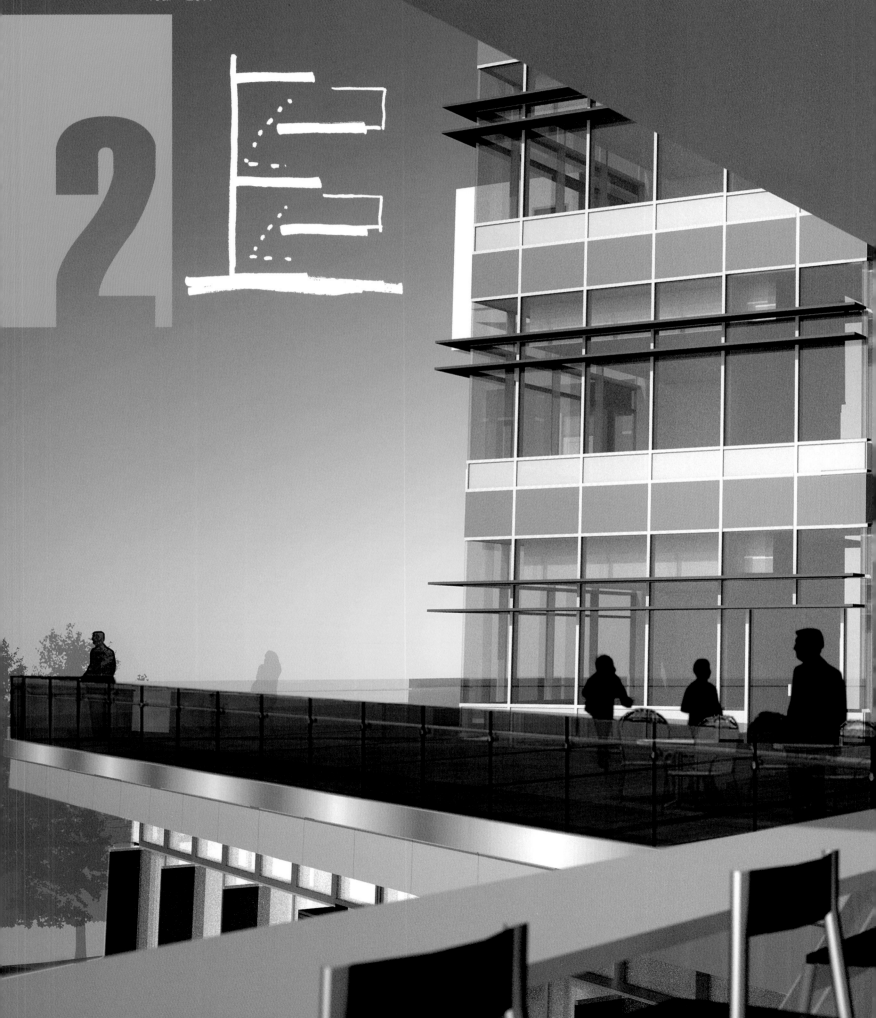

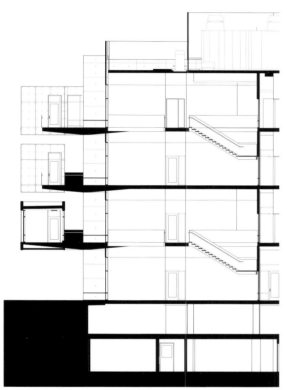

FLOOR PLAN

Research areas in the Sanford Consortium for Regenerative Medicine are organized into pods, which offer state-of-the-art laboratory areas as well as inspiring views of the Pacific Ocean.

Research often is a solitary pursuit. Yet scientific investigation includes the concept of collaboration, the intellectual give and take that sparks ideas and untangles theories. It has only been recently, however, that laboratory and research facilities have been designed to reflect this vital ingredient in the quest for answers.

The result is the collaboratory, a means of organizing research facilities to achieve easy interaction. Fentress has been a leader in this arena, creating innovative designs for break rooms with access from multiple floors, outdoor gathering places that invite discussion and inquiry, and amenities that allow respite from cracking nature's codes.

Years of experience are evident in Fentress' design for the Sanford Consortium for Regenerative Medicine (SCRM), a collaboration of four world leaders in life sciences research: the Salk Institute for Biological Studies, the Scripps Research Institute, the Sanford/Burnham Medical Research Institute, and the University of California, San Diego. These four powerhouses have teamed up to support a facility side by side with the Salk Institute in La Jolla, in front of the Pacific Ocean and protected parkland that offers a restorative atmosphere.

"When Louis Kahn was working on the Salk Institute, he located offices so that you looked out the window at a vast ocean view. It was inspiring," says Fentress. "In the new building, you have the same ocean view, but there also are areas such as two-level break rooms, spaces connected to all levels designed to encourage interaction – a collaboratory. It helps lead to a breakthrough."

The SCRM is designed for informal exploration, to invent tools and technologies intended to advance stem cell research and discover innovative diagnostics and therapies. A one-story lobby with a public roof terrace connects a conference center with the four-story laboratory building built of cast-in-place concrete. Private office "pods" are cantilevered from exterior walkways, offering stunning views. Extensive daylighting, shading devices and displacement ventilation are among the many strategies that have put the building on track to achieve LEED Gold certification.

"In some buildings, you create emotion, and in others you encourage interaction," Fentress says. "To have a space increase interaction or build a sense of awe, that really makes architecture work."

A predominantly pale concrete aggregate provides subtle coloration to the consortium building, which includes space for research, a conference center, and innovative break rooms that invite collaboration among scientists.

Louis Kahn's 1965 Jonas Salk Institute for Biological Studies (bottom left) presents two structures that separate to form a path to the ocean. The site for the new Sanford Consortium for Regenerative Medicine stresses that same restorative link with nature and sits on parkland protected from future development.

Location **Boulder, Colorado**
Client **General Services Administration**
Year **1998**

mountains

plains

3

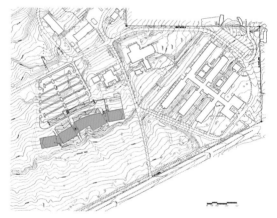

Core services and break rooms in the David E. Skaggs Federal Building are filled with light, acting as connectors for labs and enticements for NOAA researchers to relax and interact.

This segmented building appears to blend into the Flatirons behind it, expressed in stone and sunk into the land. At top, laboratory equipment offers a futuristic work setting (following spread).

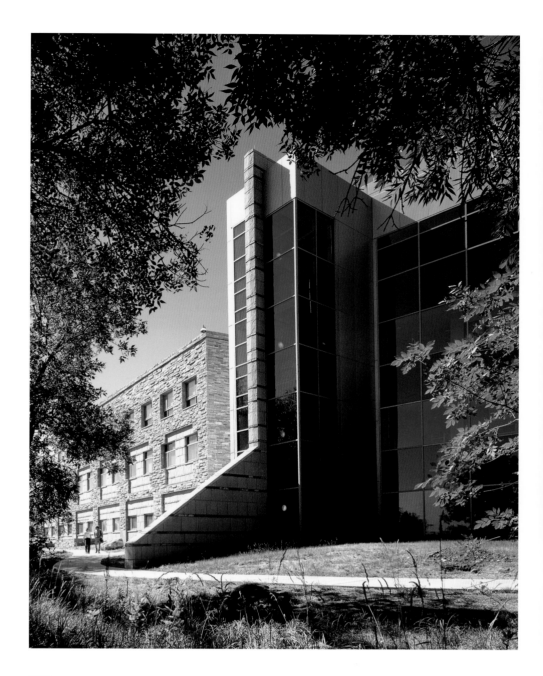

P eople in Boulder love to climb the Flatirons, a clutch of revered mountains near this environmentally sensitive college town. Building near the Flatirons, however, is a different matter: when General Services Administration (GSA) officials announced the construction of a major new facility for the National Oceanic and Atmospheric Administration's Boulder Research Group (NOAA) at the base of these sharply angled peaks, residents were concerned that the project would intrude on this scenic attraction.

Fentress' approach to designing a 372,000-square-foot building was to demonstrate respect for the site, creating a low-slung stone and glass structure that entered into a quiet conversation with the Flatirons by blending into the view.

"We angled the buildings," says Curtis Fentress. "Everywhere there's an angle, there's a silver knuckle with glass and stone in between. At that hinge point, we placed core services, including break rooms and elevators, where there are plenty of windows. That's where the scientists can get together and relax. They can get away from their data a little, and refresh their ideas with social interaction. It is the concept called collaboratory."

One level of the four-story structure is recessed into the natural grade, minimizing the perceived mass and scale and preserving sightlines. Named for a long-time U.S. Congressman whose district included Boulder, the 900-foot-long building appears as four distinct buff and red sandstone segments connected by glass and aluminum

entryways and cores. While exterior appearance was crucial, Fentress and the GSA also needed to meet the agency's demands for office and lab space, addressing energy conservation in a building with an irregular usage pattern. Numerous sustainable strategies helped prompt the GSA to name the state-of-the-art facility a prototype for new federal architecture in the January 1996 issue of *Architecture* magazine.

"Connectivity was an important issue for the researchers, some of whom at the time had hard wire connections to more than 40 separate networks within their offices," says principal Jeff Olson. "To be more flexible, a raised-floor system was used throughout the building. The nature of the atmospheric research done by NOAA at this location required that the roof be another working floor, complete with fixed observatories, tie-downs for temporary equipment placement, and operable porthole-hatches from labs on the floor below for specialty equipment."

Because of constant changes in technology, designing for flexibility is a must, as are improved safety and places for people to gather.

"In terms of the workspace and environment, there have been many changes in the procedures that make the scientists' work easier and hopefully better," says Fentress. "The opportunity of creating spaces that facilitate increased interactions of scientists is exciting to me as an architect. In a way, you are helping with the research if you can help a researcher find a breakthrough. So we continue to push the continuum of architecture. We want to create better buildings, reinvent the lab, reinvent the spaces that we use every day to be more appropriate for our modern world."

Location **Boulder, Colorado**
Client **University of Colorado**
Year **1992**

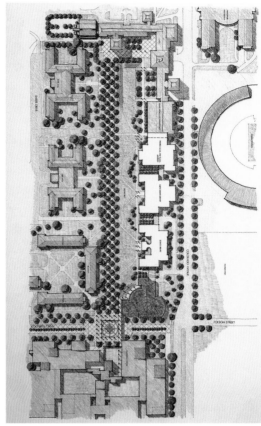

SITE PLAN

The master plan for the University of Colorado Mathematics Building and Gemmill Engineering Library stressed the inclusion of a quadrangle on the site. The space links old and new buildings in pedestrian connection with a materials palette that focuses on rustic local sandstone and Italian vernacular architectural gestures.

The University of Colorado at Boulder is known for its core campus by Philadelphia-based architects Day & Klauder, who created CU's first campus master plan in 1919 and designed numerous buildings there in the 1920s and 1930s. Even today, design review at CU stresses references to Klauder's beautiful Italian vernacular aesthetic and his use of rustic local sandstone and red tile roofs to achieve the CU "look."

Occasionally, though, designs have veered off track, ignoring the school's commitment to using quadrangles as devices both to organize the campus and create places for gatherings and relaxation.

When Fentress won the commission to create a master plan for the site of CU's new math and engineering building, he reinforced the concept of the quadrangle as an historic element in campus design, replacing a surface parking lot in the process.

The Mathematics Building and Gemmill Engineering Library includes a courtyard space that connects with the school's 1965 Engineering Center, a building that relied heavily on board-formed concrete and introduced a near-Brutalist style to campus. Nearby residence halls dating from the late 1940s were more in line with the traditional campus design approach. The math building's response to these odd couple neighbors was to incorporate some concrete, and to mark the math building with a campanile, whose sloped top referenced the angular appearance of the engineering building; the new structure's more traditional materials reached out to the older buildings with a contemporary edge.

"The public process can actually give life to a project," says Fentress. "There are so many stakeholders with so many opinions that you get the opportunity to do what's best. The bigger the project, the greater the demand for credibility that you are required to meet. This translates into trust on the job and greater creativity."

This assemblage of quadrangle and pathways was a parking lot before university officials commissioned the math building. The arcade and tower anchor a building that includes classrooms, offices, a library and an auditorium, all marked by a contemporary take on the University of Colorado "look."

5

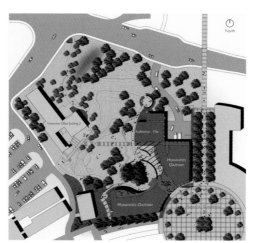

SITE PLAN

The site plan for the Humanities Gateway building illustrates the dual nature of the project, with its more formal face turned to the campus' centrally placed parkland and a more contemporary façade embracing a courtyard and expansive views. Light courts provide unexpected but greatly welcomed interior illumination.

The word "humanities" encompasses scholarly pursuits that address culture, philosophy, history, languages and the thought and innovation prized in modern civilizations.

So when the University of California at Irvine wanted to build what it termed a humanities "gateway," it was the perfect opportunity for an architect to experiment in form, approach and intent. Fentress won first prize in a national competition to design the building, following officials' directive to create a Janus-faced structure; that is, two different faces performing two different functions in the building. As with the humanities, these faces look backward, to study where we have come from and why, and ahead, to consider behavior, creativity, and the impact of our thoughts and actions.

The design tells the story. One façade is more formal and conservative, and it turns inward toward the circular park that anchors the core campus. Noted California architect William Pereira planned the campus in the 1960s and led the team that designed many of UCI's early buildings, including two existing humanities buildings. The Gateway's other face, though, is more expressionistic, a series of undulating forms with bold ribbon windows that look away from the campus into the world beyond.

The cast-in-place concrete exterior illustrates a heightened level of attention by the Fentress studio, which designed geometric patterns and sharp detailing formed by hand. This consideration of the fluid aesthetics of the Humanities Gateway demonstrates both honesty of material and intent in gestures that craft an individual presence.

Tying together these two architectural personalities are elements that bring natural light into the building, merge indoors with outdoors, and encourage the kind of interaction and discussion rooted in the humanities department's courses and programming. Walls that open, rooftop clerestories, light courts, terraces and a courtyard erase the boundaries of where and when learning takes place — whether an art exhibition, a film festival or a program of folk dancing.

"During the competition, I made a sketch on the grease board," says Curtis Fentress. "There were two faces, but they were cut from the same fabric. The courtyard, I called it the jelly inside the doughnut. Light wells become the guts of the building, and we created an indoor/outdoor pattern."

Such strategies do more than give the building a sense of transparency. They also bring natural light into the equation, reducing the need for artificial lighting and helping to place the Humanities Gateway on track to achieve LEED Gold certification.

The Gateway has become its own sort of academic demonstration project, utilizing interpretive design, history and inspiration in order to ground students in skills that stimulate intellectual honesty and the love of learning.

The undulating outward-looking façade (left) gains rhythm from segmented ribbon windows, in contrast with the more intricately detailed building and formal face Humanities Gateway presents to the campus.

LIGHT WELL SECTION

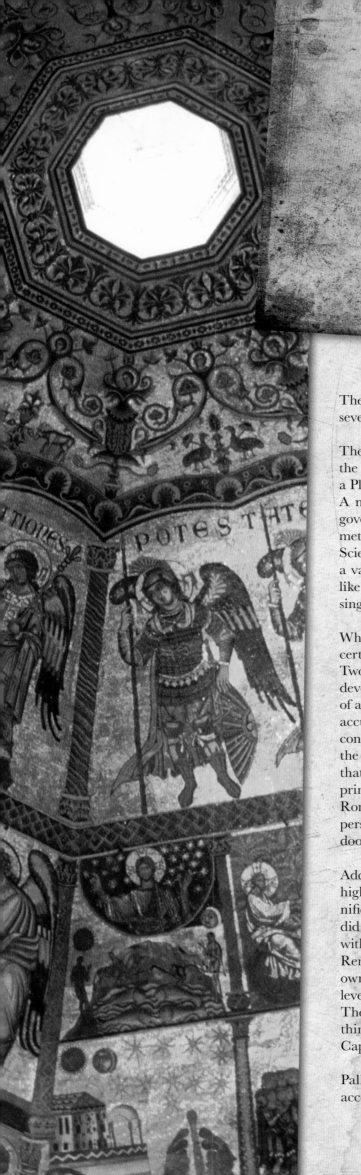

SIR ISAAC NEWTON

GALILEO

The Scientific Revolution that took place from the Renaissance through the seventeenth century occurred at a dramatic pace across a variety of disciplines.

The breakthroughs of the Scientific Revolution largely arose from a move away from the Aristotelian dependence on surface-level observations and appearances, and toward a Platonic emphasis on formal mathematical properties underlying everyday phenomena. A method of hypothesis and experiment was developed to discover the inherent laws governing the properties of extended matter. This approach was strengthened by Newton's method of composition, wherein each successive method edified the validity of the next. Scientists such as Galileo also emphasized the incorporation of established laws across a variety of disciplines: mathematics, astronomy, chemistry, biology, and physics. Much like the interdisciplinary approach of the ancient Greeks, Galileo's belief was that one singular mechanism was capable of linking all scientific disciplines.

While the Scientific Revolution didn't necessarily have its origins in architecture, it was certainly linked to theories devised through the documenting of constructed space. Two fifteenth-century architects, Filippo Brunelleschi and Leon Battista Alberti, developed the modern system of coordinates that referenced every volume, vault, or volute of a building in one integrated schema. They became central figures in the move to more accurately understand and describe the nature of reality. Brunelleschi's mathematical concept of the vanishing point (that is, converging parallel lines, which in a drawing proffer the illusion of the vanishing point) also became increasingly popular in paintings that sought to evoke realistic perspective in two-dimensional representations. While the principle of the vanishing point was popular knowledge among the ancient Greeks and Romans, it was lost in later centuries. Brunelleschi deftly demonstrated the principles of perspective when he painted the Baptistery of San Giovanni from six feet within the center door of Santa Maria del Fiore.

Additionally, the work of sixteenth-century architects such as Andrea Palladio, who was highly influenced by Roman and Greek architects, is still considered to have made a significant impact on the trajectory of Western architecture. Palladio's approach was one that did not require expensive materials (many of his edifices were built from brick and covered with stucco). His urban palazzo structure advanced the concept of the typical early Renaissance palazzo, which was both an aesthetic and functional expression of the owner and his social position. The living quarters, which typically were on the second level of the structure, were distinguished primarily by a pedimented classical portico. The height of the portico was achieved by combining the owner's sleeping quarters on the third level within a two-story classical colonnade, which was adapted from Michelangelo's Capitoline buildings in Rome.

Palladio's building format focused on a centralized block raised on an elevated podium, accessed by grand steps, and flanked by lower service wings. This style became popular

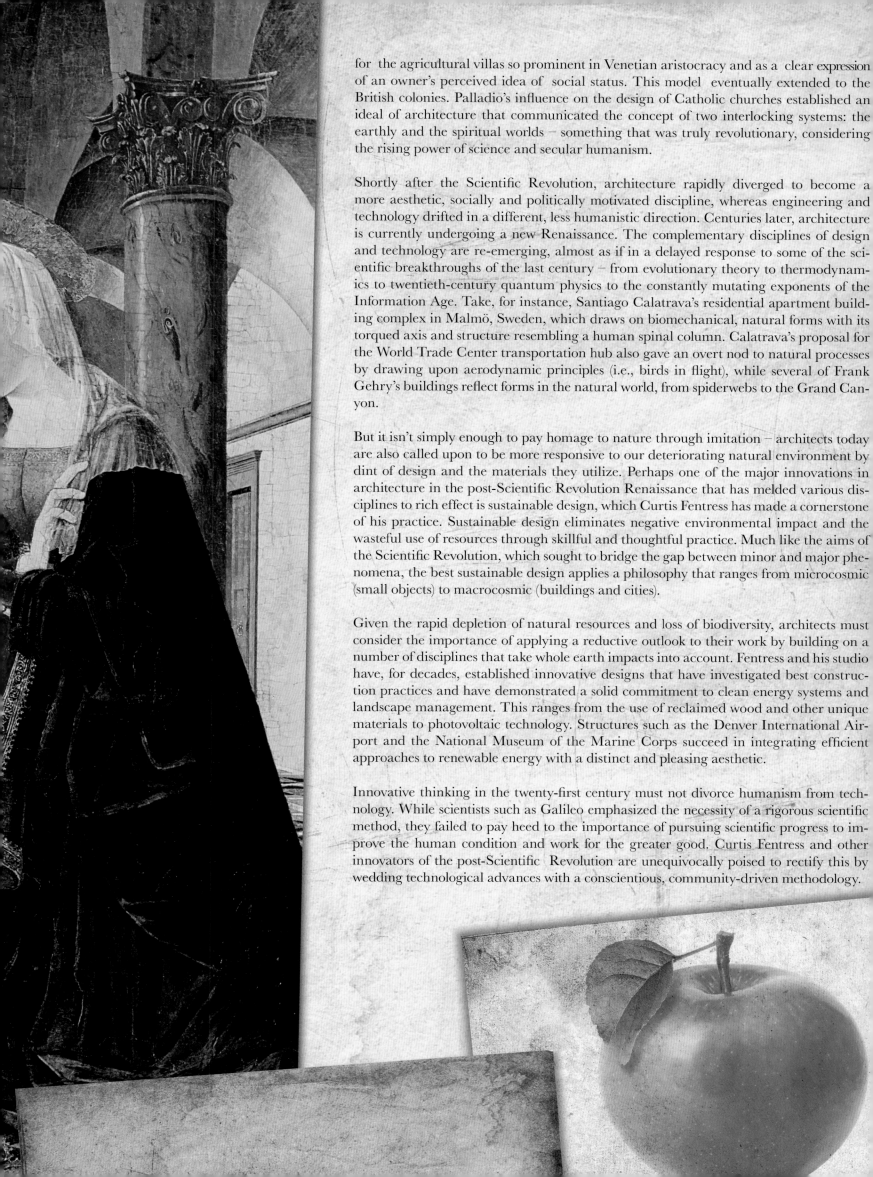

for the agricultural villas so prominent in Venetian aristocracy and as a clear expression of an owner's perceived idea of social status. This model eventually extended to the British colonies. Palladio's influence on the design of Catholic churches established an ideal of architecture that communicated the concept of two interlocking systems: the earthly and the spiritual worlds – something that was truly revolutionary, considering the rising power of science and secular humanism.

Shortly after the Scientific Revolution, architecture rapidly diverged to become a more aesthetic, socially and politically motivated discipline, whereas engineering and technology drifted in a different, less humanistic direction. Centuries later, architecture is currently undergoing a new Renaissance. The complementary disciplines of design and technology are re-emerging, almost as if in a delayed response to some of the scientific breakthroughs of the last century – from evolutionary theory to thermodynamics to twentieth-century quantum physics to the constantly mutating exponents of the Information Age. Take, for instance, Santiago Calatrava's residential apartment building complex in Malmö, Sweden, which draws on biomechanical, natural forms with its torqued axis and structure resembling a human spinal column. Calatrava's proposal for the World Trade Center transportation hub also gave an overt nod to natural processes by drawing upon aerodynamic principles (i.e., birds in flight), while several of Frank Gehry's buildings reflect forms in the natural world, from spiderwebs to the Grand Canyon.

But it isn't simply enough to pay homage to nature through imitation – architects today are also called upon to be more responsive to our deteriorating natural environment by dint of design and the materials they utilize. Perhaps one of the major innovations in architecture in the post-Scientific Revolution Renaissance that has melded various disciplines to rich effect is sustainable design, which Curtis Fentress has made a cornerstone of his practice. Sustainable design eliminates negative environmental impact and the wasteful use of resources through skillful and thoughtful practice. Much like the aims of the Scientific Revolution, which sought to bridge the gap between minor and major phenomena, the best sustainable design applies a philosophy that ranges from microcosmic (small objects) to macrocosmic (buildings and cities).

Given the rapid depletion of natural resources and loss of biodiversity, architects must consider the importance of applying a reductive outlook to their work by building on a number of disciplines that take whole earth impacts into account. Fentress and his studio have, for decades, established innovative designs that have investigated best construction practices and have demonstrated a solid commitment to clean energy systems and landscape management. This ranges from the use of reclaimed wood and other unique materials to photovoltaic technology. Structures such as the Denver International Airport and the National Museum of the Marine Corps succeed in integrating efficient approaches to renewable energy with a distinct and pleasing aesthetic.

Innovative thinking in the twenty-first century must not divorce humanism from technology. While scientists such as Galileo emphasized the necessity of a rigorous scientific method, they failed to pay heed to the importance of pursuing scientific progress to improve the human condition and work for the greater good. Curtis Fentress and other innovators of the post-Scientific Revolution are unequivocally poised to rectify this by wedding technological advances with a conscientious, community-driven methodology.

other publications on Curtis Fentress or the Fentress studio

Touchstones of Design: [re]defining public architecture . 2010 . Curtis Worth Fentress . Images Publishing

Portal to the Corps . 2007 . Edited by Jessica del Pilar . Images Publishing

National Museum of the Marine Corps . 2006 . Curtis Worth Fentress . NC State University College of Design

10 Airports . 2006 . Fentress Bradburn Architects . Edizioni Press

Museums + Theaters . 2003 . Fentress Bradburn Architects . Edizioni Press

Civic Builders . 2002 . Curtis Worth Fentress . Wiley-Academy

Architecture in the Public Interest . 2001 . Curtis Worth Fentress . Edizioni Press

Fentress Bradburn Architects . 2001 . Millennium Series . Edizioni Press

Gateway to the West: Denver International Airport . 2000 . Jessica Sommers . Images Publishing

Master Architect Series III . 1999 . Fentress Bradburn Architects . Images Publishing

Fentress Bradburn Architects . 1995 . Roger A. Chandler . Studio Press

Curtis Worth Fentress . 1995 . L'Arca Edizioni

the evolution of an architecture firm

Fentress Architects . 2007
Fenrtress Bradburn Architects . 1998
C.W. Fentress J.H. Bradburn and Associates . 1988
C.W. Fentress and Associates . 1980

More than 780 people have worked at Fentress since its founding in 1980. Their talent, contributions and commitment to inspired design for people showcase the importance of public architecture.

Agatha Kessler | Curtis Fentress   .   **art direction**

Edward W. Huang | Usana Shadday   .   **design**

Mary Voelz Chandler   .   **writer**

Jason A. Knowles   .   **photo editor**

Gabriel Ely | Matt Aune   .   **technical assistance**

Gordon Goff   .   **editor**

Andrew Cohen | Gordon Goff | John Morris Dixon | Michael McCoy   .   **contributing writers**

airports

Denver International Airport
Passenger Terminal Complex

Associate architects: Pouw & Associates and Bertram A. Bruton and Associates

"Best Domestic Airport – Gold," Leading Edge awards, *Executive Travel* magazine, 2008-2009-2010

"Best Airport in North America" *Business Traveler* magazine, 2005-2006-2007-2008-2009

America's 4th "Favorite American Architecture" landmark completed in the last 15 years, American Institute of Architects (AIA), 2007

Honor awards, AIA Denver and Colorado chapters, and Western Mountain Region, 1994

Incheon International Airport
Passenger Terminal Complex

In association with KACI (Korean Architects Collaborative International)

"World's Best Airport," Airports Council International, 2005-2006-2007-2008-2009-2010

"World's Best Airport," Skytrax World Airport Awards™, 2009

"World's Best Airport," *Global Traveler* magazine, 2006-2007-2008-2009

"Best International Airport – Gold," Leading Edge awards, *Executive Travel* magazine, 2010

Gold Nugget Judge's Grand Award, Pacific Coast Builders Conference, 2002

Merit award, American Institute of Architects, Denver Chapter, 2001

Los Angeles International Airport
Bradley West International Passenger Terminal Modernization + LAX Master Plan

Associate architects: HNTB Architects and BASE architecture

"Top ten most promising future projects of architecture in California," *California Home & Design Magazine*, 2009

Seattle-Tacoma International Airport
Central Terminal Expansion and Redevelopment

Associate architects: Streeter & Associates

Honor award, American Institute of Architects (AIA), Denver Chapter, and citation award, AIA, Western Mountain Region, 2007

Judge's Grand Award, Gold Nugget Awards, Pacific Coast Builders Conference, 2006

Editor's Pick "Best Airport," Leading Edge award, *Executive Traveler* magazine, 2009

Raleigh-Durham International Airport
Terminal 2 and Concourse Redevelopment

Associate architects: O'Brien/Atkins Associates and The Freelon Group

convention centers

Colorado Convention Center
Associate architects: Bertram A. Bruton & Associates, Harold Massop Associates, and The Abo Group

American Architecture Award, Chicago Athenaeum/Metropolitan Arts Press/European Centre for Art, Architecture and Design, 2008

Citation award, American Institute of Architects (AIA), Western Mountain Region, 2007

Citation award, AIA, Colorado Chapter, 2006

National award winner, Innovative Design and Excellence in Architecture using Steel (I.D.E.A.S), American Institute of Steel Construction, 2005

Grand Award, Gold Nugget Awards, Best Public/Private Special Use Facility, Pacific Coast Builders Conference, 2005

Pasadena Convention Center
Associate architects: Miralles Associates

Palm Springs Convention Center
People's Choice Award, American Institute of Architects, Denver Chapter, 2008

Santa Fe Community Convention Center
Associate architects: Spears Architects

Heritage Preservation Award, City of Santa Fe Historic Design Review Board and Archaeological Review Committee, 2009

museums

National Museum of the Marine Corps
Merit award, American Institute of Architects (AIA), Colorado Chapter, 2009

American Architecture Award, Chicago Athenaeum/Metropolitan Arts Press/European Centre for Art, Architecture and Design, 2008

National award winner, Innovative Design and Excellence in Architecture using Steel (I.D.E.A.S.), American Institute of Steel Construction, 2008

Merit award, AIA, North Virginia Chapter, 2008

Honor award, AIA, Virginia Society Chapter, 2007

National Museum of Wildlife Art
Honor award and People's Choice Award of Distinction, American Institute of Architects (AIA), Denver Chapter, honorable mention, AIA Colorado Chapter, and merit award, AIA Western Mountain Region, all 1996

Grand Award, Gold Nugget Awards, Pacific Coast Builders Conference, 1995

Museum of Science | Boston
In association with LDa Architects and Cambridge Seven Associates

credits

Associates + Selected Awards

commercial

INVESCO Field at Mile High
In association with HNTB Sports Entertainment and Bertram A. Bruton and Associates

Citation award, American Institute of Architects (AIA), Colorado Chapter, 2006

Merit award, AIA, Denver Chapter, 2003

Arraya Tower
Associate architects: Pan Arab Consulting Engineers (PACE)

World's Tallest Buildings Completed in 2009 – #4, Council on Tall Buildings and Urban Habitat

1999 Broadway
Merit award, American Institute of Architects (AIA), Colorado Chapter, 1990

Honor award, AIA, Western Mountain Region, 1985

Dubai Towers
Associate architects: KEO International Consultants

Grand award, "International on the Boards" category, Gold Nugget Awards, Pacific Coast Builders Conference, 2009

Citation award, unbuilt category, American Institute of Architects, Colorado Chapter, 2006

community

Semper Fidelis Memorial Chapel
Citation award for interior architecture, American Institute of Architects, Denver Chapter, 2010

Craftsmanship Award in Masonry Category for Exterior Stone, Washington Building Congress, 2010

civic + government

Clark County Government Center
Associate architects: Domingo Cambeiro Corporation

Honor award, American Institute of Architects (AIA), Colorado Chapter, 1998

Honor award, AIA, Western Mountain Region, 1997

Grand Award, Gold Nugget Awards, Pacific Coast Builders Conference, 1996

Best Non-Hotel Architecture, First Place People's Choice, *Las Vegas Review-Journal*, 1998, 1999, 2000, 2001, 2002, 2003, 2004, 2005, second place: 2007, 2008, 2009

Regional Transportation Center | Regional Flood Control District Headquarters

In association with Robert A. Fielden Inc.

Merit award, American Institute of Architects (AIA), Denver Chapter, 2001

Honor award, AIA, Colorado Chapter, 2000

Honor award, AIA, Las Vegas Chapter, 1999

Jefferson County Government Center
Grand Award, Gold Nugget Awards, Pacific Coast Builders Conference, 1994

Citation for Excellence, American Institute of Architecture for Justice Exhibition, 1990

Jefferson County Human Services Building
Honor award, American Institute of Architects (AIA), Western Mountain Region, and Merit award, AIA, Denver Chapter, both 1991

Oakland Administration Buildings
In association with Muller & Caulfield Architects and Gerson Overstreet Architects, plaza design by Y.H. Lee Associates

People's Choice Award, American Institute of Architects, Denver Chapter, 2003

Design-Build Excellence Award, Design-Build Institute of America, 1999

Sacramento City Hall
Associate architects: Santac Architecture

Legacy Award, International Partnering Institute (IPI), Ruby Level, 2010

Merit award, American Institute of Architects, Colorado Chapter, 2008

Design award for contextual in-fill, California Preservation Foundation, 2006

Natural Resources Building
Design-Build Excellence Award, Design-Build Institute of America, 1997

Honor award, American Institute of Architects (AIA), Colorado Chapter, 1996

Architecture and Energy Award of Merit, AIA, Portland chapter, 1993

Grand Award, Gold Nugget Awards, Pacific Coast Builders Conference, 1993

San Joaquin County Administration Building
First place, Project of the Year, National Chapter, American Public Works Association (APWA), 2010

First Place, Project of the Year, Sacramento Chapter APWA, 2009

Design Excellence Award, Novum Structures, 2008

California Department of Education Headquarters

Fentress Architects | Architect-of-record
Johnson Fain Partners | Master Architect and Design Architect
Dreyfuss Blackford Architects | Associate Architect

Governor's Environmental and Economic Leadership Awards, Sustainabilities Facility Category, State of California EPA, 2003

Design-Build Excellence Award, Public Sector Over $15 Million, Design Build Institute of America, 2003

courts

Kuwait Court Complexes

In association with Pan Arab Consulting Engineers (PACE)

education + laboratories

University of Colorado Denver Research 1 and 2

In association with KlingStubbins

Research 1: Citation of merit, American Institute of Architects (AIA), Colorado Chapter, 2007

Citation of merit, AIA, Pennsylvania Chapter, 2006

Award of recognition, AIA, Philadelphia Chapter, 2005

Honor award, unbuilt category, AIA, Philadelphia Chapter, 2002

Research 2: Grand Award, Outstanding Office/Professional Building, Gold Nugget Award, Pacific Coast Builders Conference, 2009

Technology in Architectural Practice, Design/Delivery Process Innovation Using BIM, AIA, National Chapter TAP BIM Committee, 2009

David E. Skaggs Federal Building | NOAA Headquarters

Award of citation, General Services Administration Design Awards, 2000

Award of merit, Gold Nugget Awards, Pacific Coast Builders Conference, 2000

University of Colorado Mathematics Building and Gemmill Engineering Library

Merit award, American Institute of Architects (AIA), Denver Chapter, 1994

Citation award, AIA and American Association of School Administrators and the Council of Educational Facility Planners International, 1993

Sanford Consortium for Regenerative Medicine

Associate architects: Davis Davis Architects

Fashion + Airports

© Stephane Cardinale/People Avenue/Corbis. March 10, 2009; Paris, France. Page 68

© WWD/Condé Nast/Corbis. October 9, 2004; Paris, France. Page 69

© WWD/Condé Nast/Corbis. March 10, 2009; Paris, France. Page 69

© Pascal Rossignol/Reuters/Corbis. March 10, 2009; Paris, France. Page 69

© WWD/Condé Nast/Corbis. March 10, 2009; Paris, France. Tony Palmieri. Page 70

© Condé Nast Archive/Corbis. November 10, 1999; London, England. Tony Palmieri. Page 70

© Toby Melville/Reuters/Corbis. June 3, 2004; London, England. Page 71

Sculpture + Public Buildings

Artist Lawrence Argent; Denver Public Library, Western History Collection, Ellen Jaskol, 2005, *Rocky Mountain News* archives. Page 120

I See What You Mean (Big Blue Bear), Colorado Convention Center, Denver, Fentress Architects, 2004: Composite material, with polymer concrete finish. Argent Studios. Page 120

Untitled, Sacramento International Airport, Terminal B modernization, Fentress Architects, 2011: stylized rabbit "leaping" into a granite suitcase with bronze hardware. Argent Studios. Page 122

Untitled, three-part sculptural installation for the University of Houston, 2010; bronze and granite. Argent Studios. Page 123

Wearable Art

Wallace Chan, © Chris Humphreys Photography, Inc.; *Zen*, opal, diamond, mother of pearl, ruby, crystal, 18K gold, titanium. Jason @ Clapper Production. Page 226

Moment of Eternity, emerald, fancy sapphire, diamond, citrine, onyx, mother of pearl. Chendra.T. Page 227

Tathagata – Heart Sutra, rock crystal. Derry Sio. Page 228

Struggling for a Way Out (top), obsidian, silver. Dannis Tang. *Butterfly Dream* (detail), obsidian, silver, copper, stainless steel. Derry Sio. Page 229

I Am Still Dancing, diamond, crystal, mother of pearl, 18K gold, titanium. Top left, Chendra. T; top right, Derry Sio. *Celestial Beauty*, citrine, mother of pearl, diamond, 18K white gold, titanium. Bottom, Chendra. T. Page 230

Soul Unto Soul (top), diamond, white agate, crystal, titanium. Jason @ Clapper Production. *Zen* (center), opal, diamond, mother of pearl, ruby, crystal, 18K gold, titanium. Derry Sio. *Deep in My Heart* (bottom), star sapphire, pink sapphire, fancy sapphire, white diamond, 18K white gold, titanium. Derry Sio. Page 231

Music + Dance + Architecture

© Robbie Jack/Corbis. Performance at the Tate Modern; November 4, 2003; London, England. Page 248-249

© Charles E. Rotkin/ Corbis. Merce Cunningham Dance Company rehearsing; September 1957; United States. Page 251

Light + Movement

Artist Ed Carpenter, Ed Carpenter Studio. Page 312

Triplet, Raleigh-Durham International Airport, North Carolina; Fentress Architects, 2010: Tapered laminated wood masts with stainless steel or aluminum fittings and laminated glass tip elements, dichroic glass in anodized aluminum extrusions, stainless steel cables and hardware.Rendering by Oanh Tran, Ed Carpenter Studio. Page 312

CrossStitch, Consolidated Rental Car Center, Sky Harbor International Airport in Phoenix, Arizona; architect-of-record TranSystems, associate design firms HKS, Dick and Fritsche, 2006: Aluminum channel, laminated dichroic glass, stainless steel cable and hardware. Ed Carpenter. Page 313

St. Mark's Cathedral Expansion, Seattle, Washington, Olson-Sundberg Architects, 1997: Translucent laminated, dichroic laminated, and kiln-fused glass, and structural steel. Eduardo Calderón. Page 314. Ed Carpenter. Page 315

Stone + Dignity

Jesús Moroles, at work on Oklahoma Medical Research Foundation, Nucleus Floor, Oklahoma City, Oklahoma, 2000. Ann Sherman. Page 334

Playscape, Fredericksburg granite, 1996, private collection. Ann Sherman. Page 335

Spirit Plaza Fountains, Chinese granites, 1998, work in progress for Changchun Sculpture Symposium, in China. Jesús Moroles. Page 336

The Houston Police Officer's Memorial, Texas granite, 1992. Ann Sherman. Page 337

Joslyn Art Museum *Riverscape*, Academy Black, Mountain Red, Carnelian and Dakota Mahogany granite, Omaha, Nebraska, 2009. Jim Williams. Page 337

Breakthrough Thoughts + Innovation

© Cordaiy Photo Library Ltd./Corbis. Mosaics on the ceiling of the Baptistery of San Giovanni; Florence, Italy; circa 1100-1300. Page 364

© Burstein Collection /Corbis. *The Annunciation*; attributed to Antoniazzo Romano; circa 1475-1485. Barney Burstein. Page 365-366

Museum Credits

James Montgomery Flagg (1877-1960) *First in the Fight*, oil on canvas, circa. 1917-1918. National Museum of the Marine Corps, Triangle, Virginia. Page 138

Chief, 1977, acrylic on canvas, 71 by 98 inches. Gift of Birgit and Robert Bateman, National Museum of Wildlife Art. ©Robert Bateman. Page 159

credits

Photography + Sketches

@ AP | WIDE WORLD PHOTOS

133 right

© Ben Tremper Photography

90-91, 96-97, 113 bottom, 117 bottom left, 150-151, 234-235, 240, 241, 242-243, 243 right, 244, 245, 246-247, 247 right

© Chip Raches

88-89, 91 bottom, 92, 93, 94-95, 95 top, 96 top and bottom left, 98-99

© Chris Humphreys Photography, Inc.

VIII

Courtesy of:

Delta Lighting Solutions, 225
Palm Springs Convention Center, 104-105
United States Marine Corps and Marine Corps Heritage Foundation, 136 bottom

© Curtis Fentress | Sketches

4, 8, 16-17, 22, 34, 48, 56, 62, 76, 80, 110, 128, 142, 152, 162, 174, 177, 184, 198, 208, 210, 218, 222, 236, 240, 244, 256, 268, 276, 280, 292, 298, 302, 308, 320, 326, 342, 348, 356, 360

© Ed Asmus

294-295, 296-297, 297 right

© Elizabeth Gill Lui

142-143, 144-145

© Ellen Jaskol

18-19-20-21 gatefold, inside back cover, back cover band bottom

© Erhard Pfeiffer

309, 310, 311

© Fentress Architects

All uncredited sketches, drawings and renderings

© Fentress Architects | Jason A. Knowles

Cover, 34-35, 37 bottom, 38-39, 44-45-46-47 gatefold, 48, 51 bottom right, 53 bottom left, 55 right, 107 bottom left, 128-129, 162, 164-165, 184-185, 186 top, 219, 220, 221, 238-239, 302, 304, 305, 306-307, 307 top, 327, 347 left, 371

© Fentress Architects | Mark Rothman

51 top right, 53 middle left and right, 373

© Hedrich Blessing | Nick Merrick

XIII, 4-5, 11 bottom, 15 top left and right, 22-23, 28, 49, 51 bottom middle, 52, 56, 57, 60 bottom left, 62, 63, 64-65, 66 left, 67, 82-83, 83 right, 100-101, 102-103, 106-107, 106 bottom, 107 bottom middle and right, 108-109, 110-111, 112-113, 114-115, 116-117, 117 top and bottom right, 118-119, 119 right, 132-133, 136 top, 138-139, 140-141, 149, 152-153, 154-155, 159 bottom, 214, 216-217, 256-257, 260-261, 261 bottom, 265, 268-269, 270-271, 272, 274-275, 276-277, 279, 280-281, 284 left, middle and bottom right, 285, 288-289, 292, 293, 295 right, 300 middle left and bottom right, 300-301, 303, 307 bottom, 308, 340-341, 354 bottom, 360, 361 right, 363 right, back cover band top

© HELIPHOTO

361 lower left, 362-363

© Jackie Shumaker

174-175, 178 top and middle, 178-179

© James Jenson

15 bottom

© James P. Scholz

58-59, 60 top and bottom right, 61, 80, 81, 87 bottom, 126-127, 130-131, 137, 138 top left

© Jamie Schwaberow | RCA Creative

8-9, 180-181, 182-183

© Jason Jung | ESTETICO

188, 189, 190-191, 191 right, 192 left, 192-193, 194, 195, 196-197

© Jeff Goldberg | Esto

30-31, 157, 158-159, 159 top, 160-161, 262-263, 282-283, 283 bottom, 284 top right, 287, 289 right, 290-291, 353, 354-355

© Ken Paul

50-51, 53 top left, 54-55, 134-135, 208-209, 211, 212-213, 215, 236, 237, 266-267, 278, 357, 358 left

© Kevin Harwell

254-255

© McCory James Photography

76-77

© PACE | Pawel Sulima

Inside front cover, 172-173, 198-199, 200-201, 202, 204, 205, 206-207

© Patrick Barta

298, 299, 300 top left

© Paul Brokering

344 bottom, 346, 347 right

© Paul Dingman

24-25, 26 top, 27, 29, 31 bottom, 32-33

© Ron Johnson

12, 84, 85, 87 top, 135 right, 273, 286, 342, 343 right, 344-345, 352, 354 top, 375

© Scott Dressel-Martin

78-79, 86-87

© Steve Craft | Corbis

2-3

© Thorney Lieberman

356, 358-359

© Timothy Hursley

6-7, 11 top and middle, 13, 14-15, 146-147, 148, 156, 258-259, 264

© Tony Eitzel | Denver Panoramic

XIV-XV, 176-177, 178 bottom

© Zoom Aerial Photography

186 bottom, 343 left

ORO *editions*

ORO editions
Publishers of Architecture, Art, and Design

Gordon Goff – Publisher

USA, ASIA ,EUROPE, MIDDLE EAST
www.oroeditions.com
info@oroeditions.com

Text printed using offset sheetfed printing process in
4 color on 157gsm premium Japanese White A matt
art paper with an off-line gloss acqueous spot varnish
applied to all photographs

ORO editions has made every effort to minimize
the overall carbon footprint of this project. As part of
this goal, ORO editions, in association with Global
ReLeaf, have arranged to plant two trees for each
and every tree used in the manufacturing of the
paper produced for this book. Global ReLeaf is an
international campaign run by American Forests, the
nation's oldest nonprofit conservation organization.
Global ReLeaf is American Forests' education and
action program that helps individuals, organizations,
agencies, and corporations improve the local and
global environment by planting and caring for trees.

North American Distribution:

Publishers Group West
1700 Fourth Street
Berkeley, CA 94710
USA
www.pgw.com

International Distribution:
www.oroeditions.com

Printed in China by ORO Group LTD.

TEAM

Abbey Williams
Adriana Zarrillo
Agatha Kessler
Agnes Wong
Al Roberts
Ala Hason
Alex Knowles
Alex Thome
Alexa Taylor
Alika Brooks
Alisha Hammett
Alvin Pastrana
Amber Stewart
André Vite
Andrew Bodley
Ann Marie Roy
Bence Kovacs
Beverly Pax
Bill Ditalush
Bill Vinyard
Bob Louden
Brandon Lucero
Brian Chalfee
Brianna Bowlin
Bryan Kristof
Bryan Smith
Carl Goodiel
Carol Carr
Carol Koplin
Charles Cannon
Charles Starr
Charles Fentress
Chris Lynch
Chris Peters
Chris Rooney
Christopher Dean-Campbell
Clover
Corey Ochsner
Courtney Hollohan
Curtis Fentress
Dave Tidey
David Hofmann
David Mecham
David Woo
Debbie Roberts
Deborah Lucking
Dee Rendon
Derek Price
Derek Starkenburg
Dylan McQuinn
Edward Huang
Elizabeth Turner
Emily Finch
Emmett Harrison
Eric Lind
Eric Zenoni
Evan Miller
Fernando Santos
Greg Billingham
Holly Carson
Ian Torres-Winters
Jack Cook
Jaclyn Wenaas
Jared Blank
Jason Knowles
Jason Loui
Jayne Coburn
Jeff Olson
Jeffrey Anglada
Jennifer Gee
Jennifer Ito
Jeremy Phillips
Jesse Dzierzanowski
Jessica Seitz
Ji-hyun Kim
Jim Sobey
John Stoltze
Jordan Roos

PUBLIC ARCHITECTURE
THE ART INSIDE

30 FENTRESS